THE CALL TO ARMS

THE 1812 INVASIONS OF UPPER CANADA

UPPER CANADA PRESERVED
WAR OF 1812

THE CALL TO ARMS
THE 1812 INVASIONS OF UPPER CANADA

RICHARD FELTOE

DUNDURN
TORONTO

Editor: Cheryl Hawley
Design: Jennifer Scott
Printer: Webcom

Library and Archives Canada Cataloguing in Publication

Feltoe, Richard, 1954-
The call to arms : the 1812 invasions of Upper Canada / Richard Feltoe.

(Upper Canada preserved War of 1812)
Includes bibliographical references and index.
Issued also in electronic formats.
ISBN 978-1-4597-0439-8

1. Canada--History--War of 1812. 2. Canada--History--War of 1812--Campaigns. I. Title. II. Series: Feltoe, Richard, 1954- . Upper Canada preserved War of 1812.

FC442.F44 2012   971.03'4   C2012-900083-3

1 2 3 4 5   16 15 14 13 12

We acknowledge the support of the **Canada Council for the Arts** and the **Ontario Arts Council** for our publishing program. We also acknowledge the financial support of the **Government of Canada** through the **Canada Book Fund** and **Livres Canada Books**, and the **Government of Ontario** through the **Ontario Book Publishing Tax Credit** and the **Ontario Media Development Corporation**.

Care has been taken to trace the ownership of copyright material used in this book. The author and the publisher welcome any information enabling them to rectify any references or credits in subsequent editions.

J. Kirk Howard, President

Printed and bound in Canada.

Visit us at
Dundurn.com
Definingcanada.ca
@dundurnpress
Facebook.com/dundurnpress

Dundurn
3 Church Street, Suite 500
Toronto, Ontario, Canada
M5E 1M2

Gazelle Book Services Limited
White Cross Mills
High Town, Lancaster, England
LA1 4XS

Dundurn
2250 Military Road
Tonawanda, NY
U.S.A. 14150

This book is offered:

First, as a salute to the memory of all those, on both sides of the lines, who served, sacrificed, and died as they loyally obeyed their country's call-to-arms in the North American War of 1812–1815.

Second, as a mark of respect to the men and women of Canada's military services, who today honorably continue that legacy of service and sacrifice at home and across the globe.

Third, as a thank-you to my fellow "Living History" re-enactors, with and against whom I've "fought" for so many years.

Finally, as a legacy for my grandsons, Anthony, Lawrence, and Daniel. The treasure of their "Bamp's" life, "junior" re-enactors, and hope for the future in the preservation and commemoration of our nation's heritage and history.

TABLE OF CONTENTS

ACKNOWLEDGEMENTS

This work would have been impossible to achieve without the support, dedication, and selfless efforts of more people than it is possible to properly credit within this space. Therefore, I must restrict myself to naming but a few, whilst saluting the many.

First, to Diane, my supporting cheerleader, chief-secretary, communications co-ordinator, and long-suffering, understanding, and lonely wife. She who has backed me all the way as I have effectively become a hermit during the course of the years it took to research and write this series. "Sorry, Pet, I promise the next one won't be so bad," has been the mantra I have used before on previous single-book projects, but now it needs to be amended to, "Sorry, Pet, here we go again — times six!"

Next, to my friend and fellow historian on the American side of the Niagara River, Pat Kavanagh, who freely and without hesitation gave me unrestricted access to his vast resource collection of American records, official documents, and personal letters on the war. Without his aid and resources, this work could not have been created. I thank you, sir.

Thirdly, I must extend these same thanks to the many dedicated staff members of the numerous museums, archives, and libraries that I visited to undertake the research for this work, who cheerfully assisted my searches to fruition and sometimes revealed previously unknown nuggets of history for me to use.

Penultimately, I cannot fail to acknowledge the guidance and support provided by the whole team at Dundurn Press in turning this idea into a reality.

Finally, I salute the memory of Karen, my friend and guide, who taught me to appreciate Canada's heritage legacy. Always my harshest editorial and literary critic, she was at the same time a staunch supporter and fiercest proponent of the value of my writings. She may not have lived to see this work completed, but her spirit and love of our history and heritage lives on within it.

PREFACE

A MATTER OF CONVERSION

To the younger generation, the metric system is the international measurement norm that has become the standard for almost all calculations. However, for older individuals like myself, the imperial system, with all its idiosyncrasies and variations, still holds true in our basic mental image of how big or how much something is. As a result, writing a book with measurements calculated in this earlier system requires some kind of conversion method if the younger reader is to "get the picture." For those wishing to undertake the exercise, there are a host of websites that will provide exact mathematical calculations and conversions. However, for simplicity's sake, the following tabulations should suffice.

Distance:

1 inch (in.) equals 2.54 centimetres
12 inches (ins.) equal 1 foot (ft.) 0.30 metres
3 feet (ft.) equal 1 yard (yd.) 0.91 metres
1,760 yards (yds.) equal 1 mile 1.60 kilometres

Weight:

1 ounce (oz.) equals 28.35 grams
16 ounces equal 1 pound (lb.) 0.45 kilograms
14 pounds (lbs.) equal 1 stone (st.) 6.35 kilograms
112 pounds equal 1 hundredweight (cwt.) 50.8 kilograms
20 hundredweight / 2,240 lbs. equal 1 ton 1.01 tonnes

Volume:

1 pint (pt.) equals 0.57 millilitres
2 pints (pts.) equal 1 quart (qt.) 1.14 litres
4 quarts (qts.) equal 1 gallon (gal.) 4.55 litres

In the matter of money and pricing, however, things become somewhat more complicated, as one has to not only understand the system of British currency that was used at the time (outlined below), but also the additional fact that the apparent pricing and monetary values given do not equate to the real, or modern purchase values, that the converted sums would represent. Although no absolute can be given, due to the number of variables involved, a multiplication factor of around fifty will come close to assessing 1812 values in terms of their modern equivalents in 2012.

Currency Denominations:

1 farthing (¼ d)
half-penny or ha'pny (½ d) pronounced "hay-p-nee"
penny or pence (d) "pense"
shilling (s)
pound (£)
guinea (G)

Values:

4 farthings to the penny
2 half-pennies to the penny
12 pence to the shilling
20 shillings or 240 pence to the pound
1 pound and 1 shilling to the guinea

Writing monetary values was done in a linear form, with the smallest denomination on the right and progressively moving up through the scale of values to the left, thus:

Two pence	2d
Four pence and a half-penny	4½d
One shilling and no pence	1/-
One shilling and eight pence	1/8
Fifteen shillings, six and a half-pence	15/6½d
One pound	£1/-/-
One pound, three shillings, eleven and a half-pence	£1/3/11½d
Eighteen pounds and four pence	£18/-/4

To further confound and confuse matters, there was also a separate North American financial system based on the decimalized dollar. In British North America this was calculated on values established at Halifax, Nova Scotia. Thus, in 1812 the standard exchange rate stood at four "Halifax" dollars to the pound.

VARIATIONS

In writing a military history and using original quotations, every author on this subject has to deal with a certain set of problems in presenting their material. First, there is the fact that in the original documents one is dealing with historical personalities, each with varied levels of education and skills of writing and spelling, not all of which correspond to our own modern forms. Second, there are the inevitable references to official military formations, regimental affiliations, ranks and appointments, battlefield tactics and manoeuvres, etc. that can sometimes appear alien to a modern reader unfamiliar with the subject. Third, there is the reality that place names have sometimes changed entirely or have gained different spellings over the years.

To address these points, this author has chosen to adopt the following position in the presentation of his accumulated materials:

On the matter of varied spellings in quotes, the material has been repeatedly checked to ensure its accuracy and is presented just as I found it in the original documents. I have therefore not included the highly distracting term [*sic*] after each variant word, as it drives me to distraction when I see it used in other works and, in my opinion, effectively destroys the integrity and meaning of the quote to me as a reader. As I see it in reading works of this kind, either I trust that the author did his job properly and the quote is accurate, or I don't and I go and look it up for myself if I'm so inclined.

On the second point, while generally recognized military terms are presented as is, some of the more archaic or jargon-type words are followed by a modern equivalent word. In a similar manner, maintaining the differential identification of military units from the two principal combatant nations (when both used a system of numbers to designate their regiments) has forced many modern writers to develop a system that will maintain a clear identity for their readers. I have adopted this convention, and within this work British Regimental numbers are shown as numerals (41st Regiment, 89th Regiment, etc.) and where required with their subsidiary titles (1st [Royal Scots] Regiment, 8th [King's] Regiment), whilst the American Regiments are expressed as words (First Regiment, Twenty-fifth Regiment, etc.)

Finally, where place names appear with a number of variants (e.g., Sackett's Harbour, Sacket's

Harbour, Sakets Harbor, or Sacket's Harbor) I have adopted a single format for each case, based upon a judgment of what I felt was the predominant version used at the time. Where names have changed entirely, or would cause needless confusion (Newark becoming Niagara and currently Niagara-on-the-Lake), I have generally gone with what would clarify the location and simplify identification overall or included a reference to the modern name (Crossroads becoming Virgil.)

In a similar fashion, in including images where there is both a period and modern image combined for a then-and-now effect, I have tried, as far as possible, to obtain the same relative perspective, subject to the limitations imposed where the physical landscape and property ownership make it possible to do so.

THE 1812 BATTLEFIELD

To anyone not already knowledgeable about the details of the historic military uniforms, weapons, and systems of drill and manoeuvre referred to in this work, the facts presented may not always make sense to the modern mind. This is not surprising, for according to the current methods of waging war, the concept of having your soldiers stand out in the open in long straight lines, dressed in brightly coloured uniforms and polished brasswork, may be appropriate for a parade square or a military tattoo. But to do it in on a battlefield, only a short distance from a similar line of enemy troops who are shooting at you, seems contradictory to the survival of the individual fighting man — suicidal, in fact! What must be understood, however, is that the battlefield tactics of the early nineteenth century were entirely different from that of the modern-day and were based on the technologies then available for weapons production.

Today, armies can sit miles apart from each other and use radar, satellite, and aerial reconnaissance, long-range artillery, missiles, and air support to destroy entire military formations in a matter of minutes. As a result, battlefield camouflage and concealment is an essential element of tactical deployment. By contrast, at the time of this story, there were no long-range weapons of rapid-fire or mass destruction. Instead, the heavy weaponry of the day consisted of heavy and cumbersome pieces of muzzle-loading cannon. Consequently, military commanders had to rely upon hauling their artillery within clear visual range of the enemy in order to pound them into submission, flight, or destruction with cannonballs — one shot at a time! In the same manner, modern combat troops carry at least one lightweight personal firearm that usually incorporates a rifled barrel, automatic loading and firing mechanisms, multiple-shot magazines, and other high-tech gadgets that produce devastating rates of fire and effective killing ranges that cover hundreds of yards (metres). In contrast, apart from units equipped with the slightly more accurate and longer-range, but significantly slower-to-load rifled weapons of the day, the standard infantry weapon for most armies in 1812 was a heavy, muzzle-loading, smoothbore, flintlock musket. This weapon had an extreme killing range of less than 250 yards (137 metres); was basically inaccurate beyond 150 yards (229 metres) and had a single-shot capability that even under ideal conditions then took at least fifteen seconds to reload. Furthermore, climatic variables, such as wind and rain, or mechanical problems (such as a dull flint, powder residues fouling the ignition system, or any one of a dozen other factors), could reduce the firing rate for a musket from a satisfactory eight successful ignitions out of ten times of pulling the trigger, to a frustrating one in ten. If one was lucky.

Because of these technological limitations, the only effective way to use an infantry force was to form the men into long lines that allowed the maximum number of muskets to be pointed at the enemy. This formation would then be marched to an effective firing range and, upon the word of command, fire a massed volley of soft lead musketballs toward the enemy; then they would go through the complicated process of reloading and firing again as quickly as possible. In response, the enemy, using virtually the same technologies and weaponry, was obliged to use the same tactics and formations in its attempt to achieve victory. This produced the classic "Napoleonic" battlefield, with lines and columns of troops moving as unified formations, firing at fairly close ranges, and generally ignoring the self-preservational method of lying down or sheltering behind a solid object to fire.

That is not to say, however, that these latter "modern" tactics were not used. In fact, the terrain and dense forests of Upper Canada encouraged the use by both opposing armies of smaller and more manoeuvreable formations of soldiers, referred to as "Light" troops. These men were trained to fight as both line infantry and as independent detachments, moving and fighting as circumstances and opportunity dictated. This style of fighting was also used extensively by the Native allies, who perhaps had a more realistic concept of how fighting an enemy should be conducted, by using hit-and-run tactics. The fact remains, however, that except in specific instances, the traditional linear and column formations prevailed as the principal functional units for large-scale military engagements throughout the North American War of 1812–1815.

Under these conditions, with contending armies standing in the open, less than 500 yards (300 metres) apart, the use of camouflage or low-visibility uniforms becomes irrelevant. Instead, it was the function of the uniform to make the wearer look taller, broader, and more imposing to the enemy. There was also the fact that the repeated firing of the weapons produced a dense cloud of grey-white smoke that, in the absence of a breeze, could thicken to the point where visibility was reduced to a few yards, creating the oft-referred to "fog of war" that bedeviled many commanders during the course of an engagement. Under these circumstances it was vital, in those days without radio or electronic communication, for senior officers to be able to correctly identify distant troop movements and maintain control of their own formations as a battle progressed. As a result, the use of distinct "National" styles and highly visible colours of uniforms provided a vital means of identification and control in the chaos of a battlefield. Likewise, the addition of highly visible regimental colours (flags), served on the one hand as a valuable rallying point for its soldiers and an indication of where a regiment's commander and senior officers would generally be located, while on the other as a perfect point-of-aim for the enemy's fire.

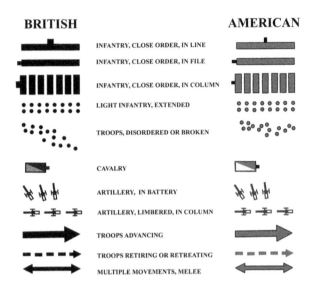

BRITISH		AMERICAN
	INFANTRY, CLOSE ORDER, IN LINE	
	INFANTRY, CLOSE ORDER, IN FILE	
	INFANTRY, CLOSE ORDER, IN COLUMN	
	LIGHT INFANTRY, EXTENDED	
	TROOPS, DISORDERED OR BROKEN	
	CAVALRY	
	ARTILLERY, IN BATTERY	
	ARTILLERY, LIMBERED, IN COLUMN	
	TROOPS ADVANCING	
	TROOPS RETIRING OR RETREATING	
	MULTIPLE MOVEMENTS, MELEE	

CHAPTER 1

Introduction

Almost as soon as the news of the signing of the Treaty of Ghent (December 24, 1814) reached the continent of North America and the conflict that has become commonly, if inaccurately, known as the War of 1812 ended, publications about the war began to appear. Some were the memoirs of an assortment of the leading military and political leaders of the day — all anxious to have their "heroic" deeds recognized and their importance within the war cast in a positive light. Others were documentary or encyclopedic "impartial" histories, which in reality usually translated as being determined to justify their own nation's reasons for fighting the conflict and to prove conclusively that their respective country had "won" the war. Finally, there were the works that established the foundation of many of the still-persistent myths about the War of 1812. These included American volumes claiming the war as America's "Second War of Independence," and that the British burned Washington, D.C., in revenge for the American invasion at York (Toronto). While in Canadian books there appeared the stories of Brock's visit to his supposed fiancé during his ride to Queenston, the substance of his famous last words as he lay dying on the battlefield, and of "How Laura Secord (and her cow) saved Upper Canada."

During the succeeding two centuries, many later historians joined the catalogue of authors writing upon this subject, with varying degrees of success and accuracy in their finished works. As a living history re-enactor of this period and interested in doing research of my own, I ended up reading many of these publications and came to the realization that for the most part, they fell into one of two general categories. Either they went to the one extreme and tried to include everything that happened at every location across North America and beyond. Or they provided a microscopic analysis of a single military event or battle, but in consequence relegated the context within which the action took place, the sequence of events that preceded, and those that followed to relative insignificance. On the other hand, what were conspicuous by their scarcity were publications that fit somewhere in the middle. By which I mean works that examined the story of the duration of the war within the self-imposed geographic limit of a particular campaign front or geographic region, but still documented in reasonable detail the individual skirmishes and battles that were fought.

As a result, in looking at the overall picture of what I prefer to call the North American War of 1812–1815, I came to a simple recognition of fact. That during the course of the war, more fighting took place in Upper Canada, and in particular upon the Niagara frontier, than in any other location or region within the whole of North America combined! And that no one in recent publishing history had tried to tell that story.

As if to reinforce the significance of this geographic concentration of fighting, my readings included an article that documented the story of the medal produced by the Loyal and Patriotic Society of Upper Canada. Originally intended for presentation to Upper Canada veterans after the war had concluded, it was unfortunately never distributed (a story that will be documented later in the series). What is interesting is that the imagery on the front face of this medal shows the geographic outline of the "Niagara" region, with the "national" symbols of the American eagle, the British lion, and, for the Canadas, the beaver, facing each other across the dividing line of the Niagara River. While complementing these images are the words "Upper Canada Preserved."

I therefore decided to take up the challenge and write the story of the war as defined by the image and words on that medal. Unfortunately, this work eventually became more of a tome of unwieldy, but well-detailed, proportions. As a result, it has been divided into a more manageable and publishable series of six chronological parts. This is not to say that I have ignored events and influences that took place beyond the Niagara frontier or Upper Canada that had an impact upon this region's campaigns and battles, for these will also be referred to, in varying degrees of detail, as the story is told.

Image from Benson J. Lossing, *Pictorial Field Book of the War of 1812*, 1868.

The "Upper Canada Preserved" medal was produced, but never officially issued, by the Loyal and Patriotic Society of Upper Canada in 1814. Originally created as a limited edition of sixty gold and 550 silver medals, most were deliberately destroyed in 1840.

SETTING THE SCENE

For the modern traveller, driving from the province of Ontario's eastern provincial border with Quebec, at the St. Lawrence River, to the international border with the United States, at the Detroit River, represents a day or so of either "zipping" along the multi-lane 401 highway or taking a more leisurely passage along the older "heritage" roads of southern Ontario. These latter routes were once the main arteries of communication and travel across country, and today consist of broad paved roads, well-signposted directions, scenic by-ways, heritage plaques, and viewing points. Not to mention a host of towns and communities where one can find food and lodgings, if needed.

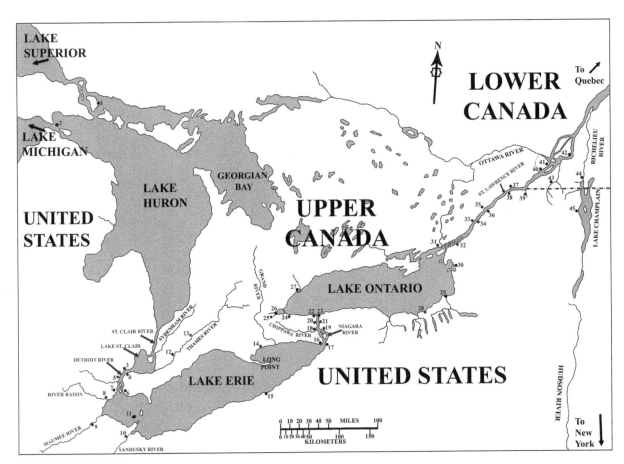

The "Northern frontier" of the War of 1812–1815.

THE "NORTHERN FRONTIER" OF THE WAR OF 1812–1815

1. St. Joseph Island [Fort St. Joseph]
2. Michilimackinac Island (Mackinac) [Fort Mackinac/Fort Michilimackinac]
3. Detroit [Fort Detroit]
4. Sandwich (Windsor)
5. Monguagon/Maguaga
6. Amherstburg (Malden) [Fort Amherstburg]
7. Brownstown
8. Frenchtown
9. Perrysburg [Fort Meigs]
10. [Fort Stephenson]
11. Put-in-Bay
12. Moravianstown
13. Longwoods
14. Port Dover
15. Erie (PA)
16. Fort Erie [Fort Erie]
17. Buffalo/Black Rock
18. Chippawa
19. [Fort Schlosser]
20. Queenston
21. Lewiston
22. Newark (Niagara-on-the-Lake) [Fort George, Fort Mississauga]
23. [Fort Niagara]
24. Stoney Creek
25. Ancaster
26. Burlington Heights
27. York (Toronto) [Fort York]
28. Sodus (NY)
29. Oswego [Fort Oswego]
30. Sackets Harbor [Fort Tompkins, Fort Volunteer]
31. Kingston [Fort Frederick, Fort Henry]
32. French Creek
33. Elizabethtown/Brockville
34. Morrisburg (Morrisville) (NY)
35. Prescott [Fort Wellington]
36. Ogdensburg
37. Chrysler's Farm
38. Hamilton (Waddington) (NY)
39. French Mills
40. Coteau-du-Lac
41. Cedars
42. Montreal
43. Châteauguay
44. Île aux Noix
45. Plattsburg

By contrast, during the early 1800s, visitors to Upper Canada saw this same region as either a virtually impenetrable wilderness, a new frontier of European civilization and settlement, or a prime location for economic exploitation of its seemingly infinite natural resources. The military and naval transport hub of Kingston on Lake Ontario was the only community of any size and importance, while the remainder consisted of little more than small towns, villages, or isolated hamlets.

In terms of development, Upper Canada's eastern border with Lower Canada was composed of a mixture of forests, relatively well-established agricultural farmland, and riverside communities. These settlements were linked together by both the main waterborne "highway" of the St. Lawrence River and a network of variable-quality roads and trails that either followed or ran inland from the river's northern bank. This type and level of development continued up the St. Lawrence River valley to Lake Ontario and Kingston. Beyond that there was a relatively less-developed corridor of farming and settlement, running along the north shore of Lake Ontario to the growing lakeside community of "Muddy" York (present-day Toronto) and then on to the smaller settlements of Head-of-the-Lake (Hamilton) and Ancaster, located at the far western end of Lake Ontario. However, beyond this point, anyone wishing to travel overland toward the Detroit River found themselves in another world entirely. Travellers who used the Grand and Thames River valleys to reach the Detroit frontier repeatedly talked about passing by, or worse through, a wilderness of forests, rocks, and bogs — interrupted only by a series of underdeveloped clearings and scattered pockets of crude frontier settlement. Similarly, they described the inland road network as consisting of little more than overgrown and rutted tracks, carved directly from the surrounding "bush," that were clogged with dust in the summer, mud in the spring and autumn, and snow in the winter.

Instead, prior to 1812, travellers looking to pass from the lower to the upper Great Lakes generally made a southerly detour that followed the line of the Niagara Peninsula, Lake Erie, and the Detroit River. Because of this diversion, the Niagara Peninsula became the primary corridor for all transportation and movement between Lake Ontario and the upper reaches of the province. In a similar manner, when the time came for the logistical planning of military operations during the War of 1812–1815, the "Niagara" became the focus of repeated campaigns to control Upper Canada and thereby determine the future of North America. Conversely, the existing physical landscape of this region and the limitations it imposed on movement of large bodies of troops and supplies also

played a major role in the determination of plans, the selection of points for attack and defence, and the course of subsequent events during the war that was to occur. As it plays a major part in this story, the physical geography of this region needs to be briefly reviewed before continuing.

Facing left: *The York Road*, J.P. Cockburn, artist, circa 1830. Part of the main road linking Kingston to York under good travelling conditions for the period.

Facing right (top): *Corduroy Road near Guelph, Upper Canada*, H.B. Martin, artist, circa 1832. A "corduroy" road, constructed of baulks of cut timber, designed to create a raised pathway for wagons to drive (bone-jarringly) through regions of wet or swampy ground.

Facing right (bottom): *Encampment of the Royal Regiment at London, Upper Canada*, F.H. Ainslie, artist, circa 1842. British troops encamp as best they can amidst the oversized stumps of the ever-present trees.

Although painted in the postwar period, these images give a good idea of what
Upper Canada looked like in the early nineteenth century.

Library and Archives Canada, C-012632.

Library and Archives Canada, C-115040.

Library and Archives Canada, C-000526.

THE PHYSICAL GEOGRAPHY OF THE NIAGARA REGION

The Niagara region is composed of a roughly rectangular strip of land some fifty miles long (80 kilometres) and thirty wide (50 kilometres), running in a generally east-to-west line between the basins of Lake Erie and Lake Ontario. It might more properly be referred to as an isthmus of land, connecting the greater landmasses to the northwest and southeast, but because the Niagara River cuts a definitive path from the eastern end of Lake Erie, down into the western end of Lake Ontario, the area is commonly referred to as a peninsula. Because the bedrock consists of intermixed layers of types of stone, ranging from the softer limestones, clays, and shale, to the harder sandstones and dolomites, the effects of erosion by weather, glaciation, and running water has produced a variety of landforms and sceneries that fall into five distinct bands.

The Lake Ontario Plain

Running along the length of the northern edge of the Niagara Peninsula at the shoreline of Lake Ontario, the plain varies in width from less than half a mile (.8 kilometres) to over seven miles (11 kilometres), and terminates on its southern border at the foot of the bluffs of the Niagara Escarpment.

Numerous rivers and streams, fed by water running north from the high ground of the escarpment, wend their way into Lake Ontario, dividing the land into a series of well-watered parallel sections. In addition, this zone has particularly fertile soils and a moderated climate (derived from the proximity of the lake and sheltering influence of the escarpment), which historically was particularly well suited for settlement and ease of movement along its length. As a result, historically, this plain became the principal land route that connected the Niagara River with the Head-of-the-Lake, the Detroit frontier, and the Lower province. It therefore also became the route along which all armies, from both sides, marched, as the various campaigns developed during the War of 1812–1815.

The Niagara Escarpment

Standing like a wall to the south of the plain rears the Niagara Escarpment. Averaging 240 feet in height, its dominating contours vary from vertical rock faces to steep-sided hills, and even today it presents the single largest obstacle to movement around the region. Breaks in this wall do occur as the numerous watercourses wend their way north and cascade off the lip of the escarpment, cutting openings that range from narrow clefts to wide valleys and culminating in the spectacular feature of

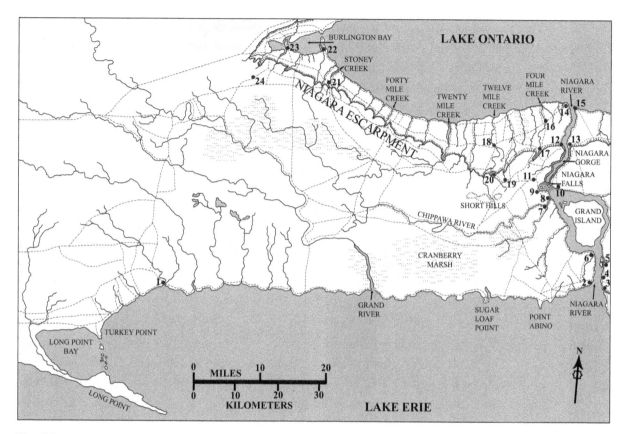

The "Niagara frontier."

1. Port Dover
2. Fort Erie [Fort Erie]
3. Buffalo
4. Black Rock
5. U.S. Naval Yard on Scajaquada Creek
6. Frenchman's Creek
7. Weishoun's Point
8. Chippawa [Fort Chippawa]
9. Bridgewater Mills
10. Fort Schlosser
11. Lundy's Lane Hilltop
12. Queenston
13. Lewiston
14. Newark (Niagara-on-the-Lake) [Fort George, Fort Mississauga]
15. [Fort Niagara]
16. Crossroads (Virgil)
17. St. Davids
18. Shipman's Corners (St. Catharines)
19. Beaver Dams
20. DeCou Mill
21. Stoney Creek
22. King's Head Inn
23. Burlington Heights (Hamilton)
24. Ancaster

the Niagara Falls and Gorge. At the time of the war, however, the escarpment created a definitive barrier that effectively channelled all military movement into routes that ran either above or below its length.

The Central Niagara Plain

Divided along an east-west axis by the Chippawa, known today as the Welland River, the Central Niagara Plain is composed primarily of extensive areas of bare rock, impervious clay, silt, and post-glacial gravels that encourage the retention of groundwater. As a result, even today it remains unsuitable for extensive agricultural development, as the numerous creeks and rivers that cross this region meander widely across the landscape, and undrained, open fields are often partially submerged following a heavy rain. In 1812, this region was considered to be impassable for military formations as, apart from isolated farmsteads, it was primarily composed of huge swamps, peat bogs, and winding waterways, only penetrated by the most primitive and narrow of trackways.

The Lake Erie Shoreline

Extending some five miles (8 kilometres) inland from the north shore of Lake Erie, the predominantly flat sand-and-clay belt of this area presents an exposed flank to the main weather systems moving up the Great Lakes basin, creating a poorer agricultural foundation that in the early nineteenth century left it lagging behind in terms of development and settlement, compared to the more fertile areas bordering Lake Ontario and the Niagara River. While it had a small road network connecting the lakeside communities in an east-west direction, the relatively easier option of sailing along the lake left these routes in an undeveloped condition, while the great wilderness of swamps and bogs to the north effectively cut it off from direct communications on a north-south axis, making it relatively impassable to troop formations.

The Niagara River

By far the most dramatic geographical feature of the region is the thirty-six-mile-long (58 kilometres) Niagara River. It leaves Lake Erie at its eastern end and cuts northward across the central Niagara Plain for about eighteen miles (29 kilometres), dropping around eight feet (2.4 metres) in the process, and therefore can be easily crossed by small boats, or in 1812 by an invading army. Reaching the Chippawa River, the Niagara River then becomes an unnavigable series of rapids as it drops some fifty-five feet (16.7 metres) over a distance of two miles (3.2 kilometres) before

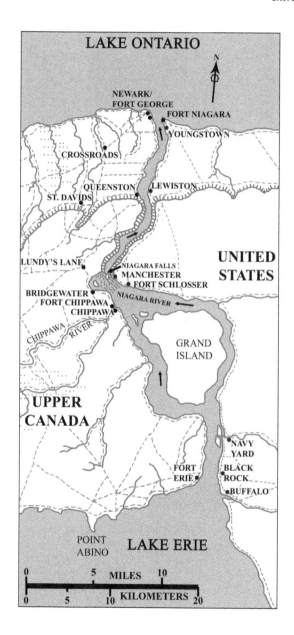

Left: Locations along the Niagara River.

cascading over the world famous "Falls" with a drop of around 170 feet (51.8 metres).

The turbulent torrent of water now enters the seven-mile-long (11 kilometre) Niagara Gorge, with almost vertical sides that reach heights of over 200 feet (61 metres) and maintain a width of about 800 yards (731 metres), making it historically a virtually impenetrable obstacle to any prospective troop movement across the river.

Dropping a further 116 feet (35.35 metres) within the confines of the gorge, the river eventually emerges from the escarpment at Queenston/Lewiston, becoming navigable once more as it gently flows nine miles (14 kilometres) across the Lake Ontario plain, for a mere eight inches (20 centimetres) of descent before finally entering Lake Ontario.

For the modern visitor, however, the spectacle of the falls is a mere shadow of its earlier natural glory, as the modern demand for vast volumes of water (to create hydro-electric power, water for the various industries, urban settlements, ship canals, and storage reservoirs) have combined to siphon off as much as 75 percent of the natural water flow that once teemed over the falls.

View of the Falls of Niagara (1801), lithograph by A.M. Hoffy, J. Vanderlyn (artist), circa 1840. The Great Falls of Niagara as seen from below Table Rock.

View from the Head of the Whirlpool Falls of Niagara, C.B.B. Estcourt, artist, circa 1838. A period and modern view, looking north (downriver) along the Niagara Gorge, around the whirlpool, towards Queenston.

View from Queenston Heights, F. Hall, artist, 1816. The strategic military importance of the commanding "Heights" on the escarpment is evident in these views. Queenston lies to the bottom left. Beyond lies Newark and Fort Niagara at the mouth of the river (upper centre), and the north side of Lake Ontario (skyline).

LIFE IN UPPER CANADA IN 1812

To understand just how different life in Upper Canada was in 1812 compared to today, one need only look to a publication called *A Statistical Account of Upper Canada* produced by Robert Gourlay in 1817. Using a series of detailed surveys and questionnaires sent out to the various townships in the pre-war period, Gourlay produced the following under a variety of headings:

It is bounded north easterly by Lower Canada, from the St. Lawrence to the Hudson's Bay: northerly by that territory: south easterly by the United States. Its western limits are unknown … In 1784, the whole country was one continued forest. Some plains on the borders of Lake Erie, at the head of Lake Ontario, and at a few other places, were thinly wooded: but, in general, the land in its natural state was heavily loaded with trees; and after the clearings of more than 30 years, many wide spread forests still defy the settler's axe.…[1]

Agriculture

Wheat is the staple of the province … [while] other grains, such as rye, maize (here called corn), pease, barley, oats, buck-wheat, etc. are successfully cultivated. The townships round the bay of Quinte, produce large harvests of pease, and generally furnish supplies of that article of provisions for the troops of the various garrisons.… The principal fruit of Upper Canada is the apple. The various species of this most useful of fruits grow in all the districts; but most plentifully around Niagara and thence westward to the Detroit where they have been cultivated with emulation and success. No country in the world exceeds these parts of the province in this particular.… Peaches flourish at Niagara … cherries, plums, pears, and currants succeed … [while] … Elder, wild cherries, plums, thorns, gooseberries, blackberries, raspberries, grapes, and many other bushes, shrubs, and vines abound.… Strawberries grow freely in the meadow, and are cultivated with success in gardens. The gardens produce, in abundance, melons, cucumbers, squashes, and all the esculent vegetables that are planted in them. The potatoe … finds a congenial and productive soil in many parts….[2]

Trade

There were, in 1810, 132 licensed retailers. At the same time there were no less than 76 licensed pedlars … Much of the trade of the country is a species of indirect barter. The merchant trusts his customers with goods, and at the proper season, receives their produce in payment, and forward it by way of remittance to the importer…. The value of copper coins is not regulated by statute … and no person is obliged by law to receive, at one payment, more than a shilling in copper money…. Most of the circulating specie is gold. Its plenty or scarcity is affected by the fluctuations of crops and markets, and the varying state of commercial intercourse with the United States. Army bills, as a medium of circulation, grew out of the war. They were substituted for specie, of which there was such a scarcity, that many private individuals issued their own notes, which passed for some time instead of cash…. There is no bank in the province….[3]

This situation is not really surprising when Gourlay reported that the hard currency of the province included the use of more than a dozen different coinages, derived from no less than eight different foreign mints, and each having its own rate of exchange.

One of the region's principal exports was furs, derived from the Native hunting or trapping of: beaver, bear, fox, otter, martin, mink, lynx, wolverine, wolf, elk, deer, and buffalo, to name but a few. In exchange for these furs:

> … the Indians receive coarse woolen cloths, milled blankets, arms and ammunition, tobacco, Manchester goods, linens, and coarse sheetings, thread, lines and twine, common hardware, cutlery, and ironmongery, kettles of brass and copper, sheet iron, silk and pocket handkerchiefs, hats, shoes and hose, calico and printed cottons &c.

These goods being ordered in the fall, are shipped from London in the spring, arrive in Canada in the summer, are made up and packed in the winter, forwarded from Montreal in May following, reach the Indian markets the next winter, where they are exchanged for skins, which are received the next fall at Montreal, whence they are shipped chiefly to London, where they are not sold or paid for until the ensuing spring. Thus is the course of this trade, requiring capital, connexions, system, and perseverance....[4]

In addition to furs, the bountiful forests provided a wealth of timber resources including:

Beech, Maple, Birch, Elm, Bass, Ash, Oak, Pine, Hickory, Butternut, Balsam, Hazel, Hemlock, Cherry, Cedar, Red Cedar, Cypress, Fir, Poplar, Sycamore, Whitewood, Willow, Spruce, Chestnut, Black Walnut, and Sassafras ... for a number of years past, large quantities of oak and pine timber have been annually cut on the banks of the St. Lawrence and lake Ontario, and its bays and creeks, and floated down on rafts to the Montreal and Quebec markets, for foreign exportation....[5]

Climate

March is the most unpleasant month in Upper Canada. The plough cannot yet move: sleighing is over: wheels sink in the mud; and the eye is out of humour with a piebald world.... During the beginning of May the leaves suddenly burst from confinement, and clothe the forests in their liveliest attire. Nature now strives amain and before June the grass may almost be seen to grow ... the autumn is equal, if not superior to that of England; and the months of November and December are certainly so.... It is the belief of the inhabitants here that their winters are less rigorous and snowy than they were when the province was first settled. A snow which fell in February, 1811, about two feet and three inches deep, was every where spoken of as remarkable for its depth....[6]

Social Life

Diversions are similar to those of the interior of New England. Dancing is a favourite amusement of the youth. Athletic sports are common. Family tea parties are the most frequent scenes of sociability. The country is too young for regular theatric entertainments, and those delicacies and refinements of luxury, which are the usual attainments of wealth. Dissipation, with her fascinating train of expenses and vices, has made but little progress on the shores of the lakes.... In winter great use is made of sleighs; and sleighing parties are fashionable; but taverns and provisions for travellers are, in many parts of the country, quite indifferent. The improvement of travelling accommodations has been retarded by the preference given to passages by water, during the summer months ... fishing is a common amusement, easily connected with occasional supplies of provision.... Fashions of dress and modes of living are common to the inhabitants of the lower province and their neighbours in the States.... The habit of smoking is very common among all classes of people throughout the province....[7]

CHAPTER 2

Beating the Drums for War

For Great Britain, the first years of the nineteenth century were extremely turbulent and troubled. The kingdom had been at war with France since February 1793 (except for the illusory Peace of Amiens of 1802–3); and this "Long War," as it was called, had, by 1812, brought the nation to the brink of bankruptcy as it sought to pay for its on-going military policies. These included:

- Constructing, maintaining, supplying, and crewing the world's largest navy in order to dominate and control the world's shipping lanes.
- Expanding its army to some 207 battalions of full-time "Line" regiments. On top of which were the seven battalions of The Brigade of Guards, three regiments of The Household Cavalry, forty-three corps of "Heavy" (Hussar)

and "Light" (Dragoon) cavalry, ten Royal Artillery battalions, The Royal Horse Artillery, three battalions of The Royal Marines, The Rocket Troop, The Corps of Royal Artillery Drivers, The Field Train of the Ordnance, The Royal Engineers, The Royal Sappers and Miners, The Commissariat Corps, The Royal Waggon Train, thirteen "Royal Veterans" battalions, nine "Garrison" battalions, and more than twenty foreign "Allied" regiments. Plus an entire additional strata of military formations, under the auxiliary militia system that raised and maintained an uncounted number of "Colonial," "Fencible," and "Yeomanry" militia regiments or battalions, "Volunteer" corps or companies, "Armed Ward Associations," "Sharp Shooter," and "Independent" companies of infantry, cavalry, and artillery. To name but a few.

- Undertaking the construction, repair, maintenance, garrisoning, and supplying of a worldwide inventory of more than ten thousand military depots, fortifications, camps, and posts of various sizes and function.
- Fighting in a series of military campaigns of dubious strategic value that frittered away vast stocks of weapons and military supplies, not to mention the lives of tens of thousands of its soldiers, before finally concentrating upon evicting Napoleon's armies from Portugal and Spain in 1808.
- Spending huge fortunes to subsidize its wavering European allies in a succession of military coalitions, initially against France's Revolutionary governments and latterly against Emperor Napoleon Bonaparte's goal to create a European empire.

As if this was not enough, Britain's domestic economy was also in a state of crisis, the combined effect of a multi-year economic depression and a succession of agricultural crop failures. This had resulted in rampant price inflation and widespread food shortages throughout the nation's increasingly urbanized population, which in turn created widespread social unrest. Compounding this already volatile situation, Britain's industrial sector

was in the midst of an ideological (and sometimes actual) conflict between its factory owners, who saw the future being dominated by the introduction of increased levels of mechanization into their industries, and their workforce, who saw their economic security, traditional working lifestyle, and their individuality being forcibly stripped away by the soulless "factory" system. Inevitably, without compromise and cooperation, both sides eventually resorted to extremes of action. The owners by invoking the "law" to call out the judges and local militias to arrest or actively (violently) suppress the protesting workers. The workers by forming raiding parties to sabotage and destroy the hated machines under the collective disguise of being the "Luddite army" or "Luddites," led by the fictitious General Ludd. As a result, the British government was already fully occupied in its own affairs at home and in Europe, and took little time to take notice of new, serious problems developing in its relationship with the United States.

The westward expansionist policies of the U.S. government had allowed white settlement into the previously off-limits treaty lands held by the Native tribes of the Ohio, Michigan, and Kentucky regions. These treaty-breaking incursions had inevitably been met with hostile resistance from the Natives, resulting in the sending in of U.S. military units to suppress the "savages." The only problem being that these same Native tribes were regularly winning these encounters! Since it was unthinkable that any "modern" army could be defeated by these "primitive" tribesmen, there had to be another reason. And as far as Mr. Grundy, the congressional representative for Tennessee and member of the Foreign Relations Committee, was concerned, the answer — and solution — was obvious.

It cannot be believed by any man who will reflect that the savage tribes, uninfluenced by other powers, would think of making war on the United States. They understand too well their own weakness, and our strength. They have already felt the weight of our arms; they know they hold the very soil on which they live as tenants at sufferance. How, then, Sir are we to account for their late conduct? In one way only; some powerful nation [Great Britain] must have intrigued with them and turned their peaceful disposition towards us into hostilities ... I therefore infer that if British gold has not been employed, their baubles and trinkets and the promise of support and a place of refuge if necessary have had their effect.... This war, if carried on successfully, will have its advantages. We shall drive the British from our Continent — they will no longer have an opportunity of intriguing with our Indian neighbours ... that nation will lose her Canadian trade, and, by having no resting place in this country her means of annoying us will be diminished.

(November 1811)[1]

For other American politicians and hardline nationalists, this viewpoint simply stated what they too had believed for some time. That the continued existence of a British colonial influence on the continent of North America was a stain on American pride that cried out for immediate correction. Their ultimate goal was to establish a single unified country, stretching from the frozen northern wastes to the tropical beaches of the Gulf of Mexico. Less often mentioned, however, were a number of financial considerations that also held considerable influence in the drive to expel the British from North America.

Under Napoleon Bonaparte, France's armies had occupied or gained control over most of the European landmass, while the British literally "ruled" the waves, thanks to the might of its Royal Navy. Because neither side could then decisively defeat the other militarily, both combatants chose to use economic warfare as an alternate weapon. The French made the first move by imposing their authority and intimidating the small Baltic states to cut off the vital timber resources of that region to the British navy. In response, Great Britain began to develop the St. Lawrence River corridor as a new and reliable source of timber from the seemingly infinite stocks of Canada's wilderness. This, in turn, represented an economic threat to the established mercantile interests on the American east coast. Within that circle it was argued that rather than seeing a competitor flourish, bringing those valuable economic resources and raw materials under direct American control would be a desirable and profitable outcome.

Matters intensified further when Napoleon Bonaparte tried to extend his economic war on Great Britain by issuing imperial decrees at Milan (1806) and Berlin (1807). By the terms of these declarations, Great Britain was banned from trading directly with any of France's allies and subjugate countries in Europe. In retaliation, Great Britain's Royal Navy effectively swept the French merchant marine from the seas before establishing a total naval blockade of French-controlled European ports. To circumvent these actions, both sides began to use intermediary and neutral shipping — a profit-making situation the Americans were quick to exploit.

Having gained control of most of the trans-Atlantic shipping trade and reaping huge profits from both sides of the European conflict, the Americans found their effective monopoly threatened by the subsequent actions of both Britain and France to tighten the economic "noose" on their enemy. Inevitably, the domestic pressure to maintain their new economic advantage, coupled with a political determination not to bow to any foreign decrees, led the American government into direct confrontation with both countries. However, while the actions of both combatants had severe economic impacts on the United States, the American newspapers repeatedly highlighted those incidents that involved British interests, leading to strident demands for retribution by the more extreme members of the American government.

In an offshoot to this situation, the huge growth in American mercantile traffic created an increased demand for experienced sailors to crew the ships. American merchant navy pay rates rose dramatically, leading to an increase in the numbers of men deserting from the brutality of the Royal Navy to the relatively lenient American trading vessels. Determined to recover these deserters, and rejecting the concept of any British citizen having the right to ever relinquish or change his nationality, the Royal Navy strained maritime legalities to breaking point by stopping and boarding

American vessels to search for and seize what they deemed to be British nationals. The intimidation finally reached its climax when the HMS *Leopard* fired broadsides into the USS *Chesapeake* (June 22, 1807) to compel her to heave-to and submit to being boarded for the purpose of being searched.

War was now a distinct possibility, and the fact that legitimate American complaints (of U.S. citizens being "pressed" into British service) were being met with blunt indifference from the British government did nothing to ease tensions. President Thomas Jefferson, faced with the difficult choice of declaring war or submitting to the demands of both France and Great Britain, chose instead to enact a series of draconian and economically catastrophic Embargo Acts that effectively quarantined the United States from all trade and business dealings with Europe. Faced with the outright ruin of their lucrative shipping industry and wholesale unemployment across all sectors of the economy, the New England region soon became the centre of a massive system of coordinated smuggling with its neighbouring Canadian maritime colonies. American customs officials were threatened and even attacked by their own citizens, as were the troops sent to enforce the new regulations. This unexpected turn of events temporarily ended the call for war, as American anger was turned inward on their own government. Although the hated

Embargo Acts were replaced in 1809 with the Non-Intercourse Act (forbidding American trade with Great Britain or France until either country revoked their own decrees), it did little to mollify the anger and concerns of the east coast merchants and shipping owners.

Meanwhile, the unremitting westward expansion by white settlers prompted the affected Native nations to unite in a common political and military confederacy under the leadership of a charismatic Shawnee chief, Tecumseh (Leaping Panther), and his brother Lolawauchika (Open Door), otherwise known as "The Prophet." In response, Governor William H. Harrison of the Indiana Territory instigated a military campaign that resulted in the defeat and destruction of the Native alliance at the Battle of Tippecanoe (November 7, 1811). From this point on, many of the surviving Native tribes became the deadly enemy of the United States and saw any potential enemy of the new republic as an ally to be secured.

The potential for conflict between Great Britain and the United States deepened in 1810, when American congressional elections resulted in the election of several vehemently anti-British representatives. Later styled "War Hawks," these politicians quickly gained control of several prominent administrative committees. They also pushed through a series of measures that could be interpreted as

The Shawnee War Chief, Tecumseh (Leaping Panther). Artist unknown. The lynchpin of the Native alliance opposing the westward expansion of the Americans in the pre-war period, he was also a crucial element in Upper Canada's defense during the War of 1812. He was killed in action against the Americans at Moraviantown, Upper Canada, in October 1813.

From *Pictorial Field Book of the War of 1812.*

being deliberately aimed at creating an atmosphere of crisis that would bring about a declaration of war against Great Britain. Using the claim of "Free Trade and Sailors Rights" as their basis for complaint, they manipulated public opinion by making inflammatory speeches and publishing vitriolic editorials in the nation's press. At the same time, if anyone questioned or opposed their position, they were immediately stigmatized with accusations of being subversive or even traitorous in their actions. As a result, the War Hawks successfully marginalized the conflict issues with France and characterized Britain, led by Spencer Perceval (holding the dual roles of prime minister and Chancellor of the Exchequer), as a villainous bully that needed to be taught a lesson.

Such was the depth of anti-British rhetoric within the American legislative assembly that Peter B. Porter, a leading War Hawk from Buffalo, New York, and chairman of the Committee of Foreign Relations, was able to openly state on December 6, 1811:

> The Committee … were satisfied … that all hopes of accommodating our differences with Great Britain by negotiation must be abandoned … the Orders in Council … ought to be resisted by war…. That we can contend with Great Britain openly and even handed on the element

where she injures us, it would be folly to pretend. Were it even within our power to build a navy which should be able to cope with her, no man who has any regard for the happiness of the people of this country would venture to advise such a measure … but, Mr. P. said, there was another point where we could attack her, and where she would feel our power more sensibly. We could deprive her of her extensive provinces lying along our borders to the north. These provinces were not only immensely valuable in themselves, but almost indispensable to the existence of Great Britain, cut off as she now is in a great measure from the north of Europe.… In short, it was the determination of the committee to recommend open and decided war — a war as vigorous and effective as the resources of the country and the relative situation of ourselves and our enemy would enable us to prosecute.[2]

However, despite every effort to create a unified national cry for war against Great Britain, the War Hawks found that when matters finally came to a formal vote for the declaration of war in 1812, the United States was still anything but united in

its position. Divided by party politics, there were also strong regional opinions for and against a war. For example, the northeastern seaboard states (Massachusetts [including Maine], Rhode Island, Connecticut, New York, and Delaware), rejected war in the Congressional vote of June 4, 1812, and submitted formal petitions of objection to the president. On the other hand, the inland states of Kentucky, Tennessee, and Ohio voted in favour, backed by New Hampshire, Vermont, Pennsylvania, Maryland, Virginia, North Carolina, South Carolina, and Georgia. Similarly, the Senate was divided in its vote of June 17, 1812. Faced with this national division, President James Madison initially hesitated to sign the bill. However, when news arrived that a lone gunman had assassinated Prime Minister Spencer Perceval in the House of Commons on May 11, and that the British government was consequently in a state of turmoil, President Madison moved quickly and signed the declaration of war on June 18, 1812.

If the American nation was not politically united in its desire for war, neither was it militarily ready to press its point by force of arms. Despite the fact that Congress had taken the president's earlier request for the raising of 10,000 regulars and 50,000 militia (November 1811) and expanded it to read 25,000 regulars, 50,000 militia, and additional funding of $10 million, it could not simply make

U.S. President James Madison (artist unknown) signed the declaration of war against Great Britain on June 18, 1812.

Courtesy of the Buffalo and Erie County Historical Society Research Library, Buffalo, NY.

I would take the whole continent from them and ask them no favors…. I wish never to see a peace till we do,"[3] and Secretary of War William Eustis, "We can take the Canada's without soldiers; we have only to send officers into the provinces, and the people, disaffected towards their own government, will rally round our standard,"[4] were flights of fancy, geared to grab the newspaper headlines. In reality, despite the prospect of war having been prophesied and called for since 1807, the U.S. military supply and distribution system was a total shambles and completely incapable of making or moving the vast amounts of materiel required on the frontiers to prosecute a successful offensive campaign:

> The keeper of the stores will not part with cannon, muskets, ammunition, or other articles, without the order of his superior officer. General Dearborn has requested me to order out the Militia … and informs me that the Quartermaster General will supply camp equipage for them. Upon application to the Quartermaster General, who is now in Albany, I find there is no camp equipage except a few tents and about sixty camp kettles which have been in our arsenal at this place for several years. For the delivery of even these I cannot obtain a written order. The Deputy

these troops appear on the battlefield. Grandiose claims of an instant victory once war was begun were made by people like Congressman Henry Clay, "… it is absurd to suppose we shall not succeed in our enterprize against the enemy's provinces … I am not for stopping at Quebec, or anywhere else, but

Quartermaster General will not give an order for their delivery without written directions from the Quartermaster General and the Quartermaster General does not seem willing to give such written directions … although he is perfectly willing I should have the articles. Under such circumstances, I shall presume to take possession of them at my own hazard and shall accordingly forward them to-morrow morning, hoping that my proceedings on the emergency will be approved and confirmed.[5]

— New York State Governor, Daniel D. Tompkins to Secretary of War William Eustis, June 27, 1812

conduct a war in any coherent fashion as long as they were led by officers who saw their military service principally as a platform for their own political advancement (and, conversely, as an opportunity to undermine any officer who was also a political rival). Finally, since senior appointments to the command and staff of the army were the individual prerogative of the president, he chose to rely heavily upon aging and sometimes infirm veterans of the revolution to lead the army. For example, the "first major general" of the United States Army, Henry Dearborn, was no less than sixty-one years old, while his fellow generals averaged fifty-five years of age. Nor were matters much better at the level of district and regimental commanders, as most had little or no actual military experience other than their ceremonial and depot duties in the pre-war period.

The official account of having some twenty-five regiments of regular infantry, four of artillery, two of cavalry, and one of rifles, for an impressive total of over 35,000 regular troops, translated into a reality of nearer 13,000 men, scattered across the entire country and made up primarily of untrained and barely outfitted raw recruits. Similarly, the springtime call for the mustering of the state militias had been a resounding failure, with many units fielding more officers than men. Furthermore, even where units had assembled, few were in a position to

Sir … I take the command of the troops at Black Rock and its vicinity in obedience to Your Excellency's order with the greatest diffidence, having no experience of actual service. My knowledge of the military art is limited; indeed, I forsee numberless difficulties and occurrences which will present to which I feel totally inadequate. I have been ambitious that the regiment and brigade which I have commanded should be distinguished at

General Henry Dearborn, (artist unknown) the senior American general at the commencement of the war. He was a veteran political appointee and relic of the Revolutionary conflict of nearly forty years previous.

Courtesy of the Buffalo and Erie County Historical Society Research Library, Buffalo, NY.

their reviews, but I confess myself ignorant of even the minor duties of the duty you have assigned me, and I am apprehensive that I may not only expose myself but my Government. Any aid which Your Excellency may think proper to order will be received with thanks. A military

secretary intimately acquainted with the details of camp duty would be of great service to me …[6]

— Brigadier General William Wadsworth to New York State Governor Tompkins, June 28, 1812

On the other hand, if the United States was in no position to begin a war, the Crown colonies of British North America were in no better shape to defend against one. Canada, except as a name, did not exist, while British North America was not a unified country. Instead, it was a collection of individual colonies, each with its own governmental body and different attitudes toward the prospect of conducting a war with the United States. Furthermore, its population was not only dispersed over a huge geographical area, but was also far smaller than that of the U.S. Estimates place the population of the combined colonies of New Brunswick, Nova Scotia, Lower and Upper Canada at less than 500,000, while that of the United States was in excess of 7.5 million. Of this 500,000, Upper Canada had less than 77,000 settlers, of which only around 9–10,000 were on the Niagara frontier. Secondly, in the event of war, while the British army had an official complement of some 10,000 regular and provincial or "Fencible" troops stationed

REGIMENTS STATIONED IN BRITISH NORTH AMERICA, JULY 1812[7]

British Regular Infantry
8th (King's) Regiment
41st Regiment
49th Regiment
99th Regiment
100th Regiment
103rd Regiment
104th Regiment (formerly the New Brunswick Fencible Regiment)
10th Royal Veterans Battalion

"Canadian" Fencible Infantry
Royal Newfoundland Fencible Regiment
Canadian Fencible Regiment
Nova Scotia Fencible Regiment
Glengarry Light Infantry Fencible Regiment

British Artillery
Royal Artillery Regiment (detachments from the 2nd, 4th, 5th, 7th Battalions)

Upper Canada's senior military commander, Major General Isaac Brock, were refused or excused away by his superior, Sir George Prevost, as being impossible to accomplish or threatening the security of the Lower colonies.

Instead, following the directives emanating from England to maintain a defensive posture and minimize the need for troops and supplies in the Canadian colonies, Prevost withheld these vital resources from Upper Canada and considered the region as expendable to the greater war effort. He also handicapped his military commanders with the following instructions:

> My sentiments respecting the mode of conducting the war on our part ... [must be] suited to the existing circumstances, and as they change so must we vary our line of conduct, adapting it to our means of preserving entire the King's Provinces ... Our numbers would not justify offensive operations being taken, unless they were solely calculated to strengthen a defensive attitude ... I consider it prudent and politic to avoid any measure which can in its effect have a tendency to unite the people in the American States.... Whilst division prevails among them, their attempts on these Provinces will be

within British North America,[7] the dominance of defensive military thinking meant that securing Halifax, Quebec, and Montreal used up almost 80 percent of the available troops, artillery, ammunition, and supplies. By contrast, Upper Canada was defended by little more than 1,200 officers and men, scattered along a defensive frontier of over 1,000 miles. Repeated pleas for additional manpower and supplies for the defence of Upper Canada, sent by

Major General Sir Isaac Brock K.B., G.T. Berthon, artist, circa 1883. In 1812, Isaac Brock held the cumulative titles of senior military commander for Upper Canada, lieutenant-governor of Upper Canada and president of the Upper Canada Executive Council. News of his knighthood only arrived in Canada following his death.

Archives Ontario, Acc. 694158.

Sir George Prevost, S.W. Reynolds, artist, date unknown. Appointed governor-in-chief and commander-in-chief of the British forces in British North America in 1811, Sir George proved to be an able civil and political administrator. Unfortunately, his on-field military command capabilities were not as strong. Following flawed decisions made during the Plattsburg campaign of 1814, he was recalled to England at the end of the war to face a court martial inquiry. He died a month before the inquiry began.

Library and Archives Canada, C-19123.

feeble, it is therefore our duty carefully to avoid committing any act which may, even by construction, tend to unite the Eastern and Southern States, unless by its perpetration we are to derive a considerable and important advantage....

— Sir George Prevost, Montreal, July 10, 1812[8]

A constraint that Brock fortunately chose to interpret with a large degree of flexibility when it came to his course of action over the next few months.

Nor did Brock receive any significant assistance from the local provincial legislature, which was salted with several actively pro-American sympathizers. This situation had arisen during the period following the colonial rebellion of the American eastern seaboard states in 1776. At that time the population of the thirteen colonies had become divided into what were termed "Rebels" (who sided with those fighting for independence in what became known as the American Revolution), and "Loyalists" (who had fought for the king). With the victory of the rebels and the creation of the United States of America, the postwar punitive measures (including property seizures and revocation of civil liberties, rights of property, employment, and legal standing, not to mention mob violence and lynchings) that were heaped upon the Loyalists forced huge numbers of individuals and families to become homeless refugees. For the British government, the plight of the Loyalists required some form of recompense. In response, large tracts of land were granted to Loyalists in the undeveloped regions of its Canadian colonies, including Upper Canada, in particular along the Niagara frontier. As a result, during the last decade of the eighteenth century, while many waterside areas saw varying degrees of clearing and settlement by these transplanted refugees, the interior of the region still remained relatively untouched. However, during the following years, increasing numbers of Americans also arrived and took up residence, bringing with them their republican sentiments. This new pro-American influx naturally generated resentment within the established communities of the old Loyalist families and their descendants, and effectively split the population into rival political camps. It also created security problems for the limited number of British regular military forces detailed to defend the border against any future American aggression. Numerous letters and reports by successive lieutenant governors of Upper Canada recorded their unease at the increasing influence and dissenting opinions of that sector of the population who maintained that their allegiance was to the United States, not the king, and who considered the annexation of Upper Canada by the United States as merely a matter of time, or opportunity.

Now, with war in the offing, these near-traitors, in the opinion of Brock and his military subordinates, were taking every opportunity to block any legislation or expenditure designed to improve the defences of the colony. In a letter to Sir George Prevost, penned on February 25, 1812, Brock commented:

> I had every reason to expect the almost unanimous support of the two branches of the Legislature to every measure the Government thought necessary to recommend; but after a short trial I found myself egregiously mistaken in my calculations…. The great influence which the vast number of settlers from the United States possess over the decisions of the Lower House, is truly alarming, and ought by every practical means to be diminished….[9]

Similarly, the Upper Canada militias, which although officially listing some 11,000 men of eligible age for military duty in the event of war, were of such a poor quality and in some cases of dubious loyalty that Prevost stated, "… it might not be prudent to arm more than 4000."[10] Instead, it was recognized that the future security of Upper Canada might depend upon the tenuous alliance of the Native tribes to the British cause. Unfortunately, here too there was a lack of unity amongst the Native nations on the desirability to aggressively pursue a war. In the upper lakes region the western tribes of the Sioux, Winnebagos, and Menominis were fervent in their desire to revenge themselves for the recent incursions of Americans into their territories. On the other hand, on the Niagara frontier the bands of the Six Nations around the Grand River were far more reluctant to go to war, and even withheld any official promise of future assistance to the British cause if the Americans attacked. Their only offer of support came by approving the use of individual warriors volunteering to act with their British allies.

CHAPTER 3

The Opening Round, June to August 1812

Following the official public declaration of war in Washington on June 19, 1812, events began to occur at an increasing pace as notices were dispatched to the frontiers by a series of messengers. Unfortunately for the Americans, although editorials on the imminence of war had filled the pages of the nation's newspapers for months, once it began the more efficient British communications network notified their distant garrisons before their American counterparts had heard the news. This led to the opportunity for enterprising British and Canadian troops to engage in some pre-emptive strikes. For example, on June 29, at the eastern end of Upper Canada, a detachment of militia stationed at Prescott saw eight U.S. vessels passing upriver on the St. Lawrence, headed for Lake Ontario. Using a number of bateaux and longboats, the detachment chased the American vessels, intercepting them near Elizabethtown (later renamed Brockville). The schooners *Sophia* and *Island Packet* were boarded, captured, and subsequently burnt, while the remaining six American boats fled back to their base at Ogdensburg, becoming prisoners in their own port. In a similar fashion, on June 27, two longboats filled with around forty militiamen and regulars from Fort Erie were able to intercept the schooner *Connecticut* as it set sail on Lake Erie from Buffalo for Detroit. While at the other end of that lake, men from the Provincial Marine, accompanied by six soldiers from Fort Amherstburg (also known as Fort Malden), used a longboat to pursue, catch, and board the American schooner *Cuyahoga Packet.* Taking the vessel into the harbour at Amherstburg, they found that not only had they captured a detachment of thirty American troops, but also a cargo of food, medical supplies, entrenching tools, and baggage. This material had only been put on board the vessel the previous day and was part of a consignment accompanying Brigadier General William Hull's army in its march from Dayton, Ohio, to garrison Detroit. While the supplies were a welcome addition to the depleted

reserves of the British force, the captors also discovered that they had gained a huge intelligence coup in the form of a chest containing Hull's entire personal and official correspondence. This included instructions for General Hull from the American secretary of war, the muster rolls of manpower for his command, and a complete set of lists detailing the quantities of ammunition, arms, and other supplies accompanying the army in its march to Detroit.

Further north, the isolated garrison at St. Joseph Island, located at the head of Lake Huron, learned of the declaration of war on July 8. The garrison's commander, Captain Charles Roberts (10th Veteran Battalion) acted immediately by organizing a lightning pre-emptive strike against the far more strategically advantageous and militarily superior American base of Fort Michilimackinac (also referred to at the time and known today as Fort Mackinac) some forty-five miles away. On the morning of July 16th, Roberts set sail in a small flotilla of longboats and canoes with a combined force of regulars, militia, and Natives, amounting to about 630 men. The following morning, before daylight, the attack force landed undetected at the northern end of Mackinac Island. Forming a column from his few regular and militia troops, Roberts flanked this force with his two large contingents of Native warriors. While at the rear, a number of men manhandled the single antique 6-pounder artillery

Brigadier General William Hull (artist unknown). The American commander at the fall of Detroit — the first of many military failures for the American war effort in 1812.

From Pictorial Field Book of the War of 1812.

Facing page: (Above): *Fort George*, E. Walsh, artist, circa 1805. The parade ground and officer's mess at Fort George in the pre-war period. (Below): A 2012 view of the reconstructed officer's mess in the National Historic site of Fort George at Niagara-on-the-Lake.

The American fortifications at the island of Michilimackinac [Mackinac] (artist unknown).

piece that had been brought along to assault the American fortifications.

Advancing along the narrow track that led to the fort, the infantry and Natives deployed into their separate battle formations, while the artillerists dragged the small cannon to a nearby piece of high ground that overlooked the fort. With his forces in place, Captain Roberts sent a note to the American garrison commander, Lieutenant Porter Hanks (U.S. Artillery), demanding the immediate and unconditional surrender of the American position. Unaware of the formal onset of war, unprepared and facing a strong enemy force, Hanks' command officially consisted of only around sixty men. Of this small number, several men were sick, while many of the remainder were relatively elderly or otherwise

considered unfit for active service. As a result, with no real alternative before him, Hanks surrendered the strategic position without a shot being fired. Tactically this victory was of only minor value, but strategically it swung the balance of power in the upper Great Lakes by securing the alliance of the western Native nations to the British war effort. It also had a decisive effect on the subsequent events that were to unfold on the Detroit frontier.

Back on the Niagara frontier, the American forces were also caught off guard. According to local folklore, when the notice of the declaration of war was delivered to Fort George the officers of the British garrison were entertaining their opposite numbers from Fort Niagara at a dinner in the officers' mess. In a show of courtesy, the American

officers were not immediately interred. Instead, the dinner was concluded with loyal toasts and expressions that a similar dinner would be held following the termination of hostilities. Following the meal the American officers were permitted to return to Fort Niagara, there to prepare for war to commence the following day.

Despite gaining these minor victories, the fact remained that the British military position in Upper Canada was precarious at best. Britain was fully committed to the war in Europe and consequently had little in the way of resources that could be spared for the North Americas. Nor could the colonial economies provide the necessary agricultural or manufactured supplies needed to sustain the war effort on their own. Even where supplies were forthcoming, they had to be transported along a long and tenuous transportation network that was constantly open to being attacked or cut by enemy action. In view of these difficulties, securing and defending the vital lifeline of the St. Lawrence River, Niagara frontier, and Detroit River corridor became a top priority in the military planning of successive British commanders in Upper Canada. Unfortunately, each in his turn had to deal with Sir George Prevost, who was seemingly willing to entirely abandon Upper Canada so that he could keep the bulk of his supplies and manpower in Lower Canada, "just in case" of an attack against Montreal, Quebec, or Halifax.

In comparison, the American war effort, while getting off to a bad start, had the strategic advantage of being waged on its own continent. Furthermore, despite logistical difficulties and equally poor roads, each of the fronts could be supplied with men and equipment by several distinct and relatively secure routes. In addition, the larger base population, coupled with a relatively strong industrial and agricultural sector, provided the resources needed to supply the armies on an ongoing and timely basis. Having gone to the trouble of declaring war, the American administration naturally looked to its military to supply it with victories to justify its action.

Unfortunately, these American laurels were not to appear for some time, as General Henry Dearborn found that his goal for an immediate four-pronged assault on the Canadas was stalled before it had even begun. His proposed main thrust (toward Montreal from Albany) failed to recruit men; while the New England states of Massachusetts, Connecticut, and Rhode Island refused outright to acknowledge the national call to arms and raised the question of seceding from the Union rather than have their men "dragged out of the State to fight Indians or die before the walls of Quebec."[1] Further inland, his planned second thrust (from Sackets Harbor against Kingston) was woefully short of weapons and ammunition, thus preventing any significant offensive from that base for some time. It was therefore up to Dearborn's commanders on the Niagara and Detroit frontiers, respectively Major General Stephen Van Rensselaer and Brigadier General William Hull, to press the American cause. Of the two, it was General Hull, who was also the governor of the Michigan Territory, who made the first move.

THE DETROIT CAMPAIGN, JULY TO AUGUST 1812

Even before war had been declared, the Detroit frontier, although the most isolated of the potential war zones, had been given particular attention by the military planners of both Britain and the United States. As early as February 1812, General Brock had set down his "Plans for the Defence of Canada." In this memorandum he outlined the vital need to secure the alliance of as many of the First Nations tribes as possible to counteract the American advantages of men and logistics. To this end, Michilamackinac was to be seized, followed by the forwarding of as many troops as could be spared from York and the Niagara to commence a direct offensive from Amherstburg against Detroit. By these bold thrusts and hopefully quick victories, Brock hoped to secure the Native tribes as allies of the Crown. In support of this, Brock made a flying visit to Amherstburg

from June 14–17, 1812. While he brought supplies and around a hundred reinforcements for the post, he also paid particular attention to solidifying the tacit pact between the Native leaders and himself.

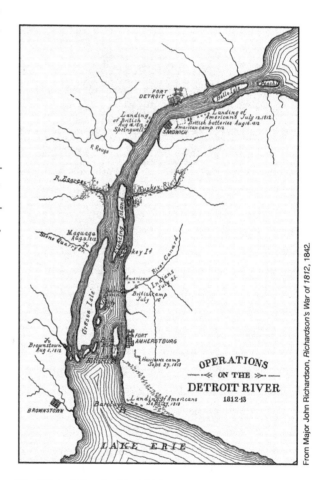

From Major John Richardson, *Richardson's War of 1812*, 1842.

The "Detroit frontier" in 1812.

He even went so far as to commit himself and his government to press for the establishment of a formal Native homeland that would act as a buffer zone between the two expansionist nations following a successful conclusion of the war.

In a similar fashion, the United States took steps before war became a reality to bolster their military position on the Detroit frontier. On May 25, General Hull was in Dayton, Ohio, massing his regular and militia forces for an expedition to reinforce the small garrison at Detroit, some two hundred miles (340 kilometres) away. By July 1, unaware of the declaration of war, Hull's army was at the Maumee Rapids, where he decided to lighten his baggage train by placing a portion of his equipment and supplies, as well as his own personal baggage and correspondence, onboard the *Cuyahoga Packet*. The intention being that they would be waiting for him when he and his army completed the journey along the shore. The next day word of the declaration of war arrived, but it was too late to prevent the capture of the *Cuyahoga Packet* and the vital stash of military paperwork by the British. Hastening on, Hull's army of around 2,500 men arrived at Detroit on July 6 and immediately set about strengthening the post's defences, while equally making preparations to conduct an offensive campaign against Fort Amherstburg, some fourteen miles (22.4 kilometres) downriver from Detroit and on the other side of the river in Upper Canada. Commanding that small garrison was Lieutenant Colonel Thomas St. George (63rd Regiment), a sixty-year-old veteran soldier of the European wars. Under his command, including the latest reinforcements, he only had around 250 regular troops. In addition, while there were, on paper, at least 600 Essex and Kent County Embodied Militia that could be called upon, most were, at best, half-hearted in their enthusiasms. Finally, there were the crews of the various vessels stationed at Amherstburg and around two hundred Native warriors under the command of Tecumseh.

On July 12th, 1812, an American invasion force of between 1,500 and 2,000 men (depending on whose account you read) crossed the Detroit River, landing a little above the village of Sandwich (Windsor). Despite the fact that there were some four hundred Canadian militia detailed to defend that position, backed by small detachments of regulars and artillery, nothing was done to oppose the landings, as the militia made it clear that if they were attacked they would retire, with or without orders! Left with no alternative and hoping to maintain some kind of fighting force, St. George ordered the withdrawal of all troops toward Amherstburg and the destruction of the bridges across the various creeks. The way was now open for a dynamic thrust by the Americans that would secure the entire western end of the province and provide Washington with its demanded victory. Instead, apart from sending out reconnaissance patrols as far south as the Canard River, and a large foraging (looting) expedition up the line of the Thames River, Hull ordered his army into a defensive posture around the village of Sandwich, still within sight of Detroit. To confirm his victory, he then sent out copies of a bombastic proclamation to espouse his role as the liberator of Upper Canada:

> Inhabitants of Canada! After thirty years of Peace and prosperity, the United States have been driven to Arms. The injuries and aggressions, the insults and indignities have once more left them no alternative but manly resistance or unconditional submission. The army under my command has invaded your country and the standard of the United States waves on the territory of Canada. To the peaceable unoffending inhabitants, it brings neither danger nor difficulty. I come to find enemies not make them, I come to protect you not injure you…. You have felt [Great Britain's] tyranny, you have seen her injustice, but I do not ask you to avenge the one or redress the other. The United States are sufficiently powerful to afford you every security … I tender you the invaluable blessings of Civil, Political, & Religious Liberty….[2]

On the other hand, he also warned of extreme retaliation if those loyal to the Crown took up arms or fought alongside the Natives, who were to be particularly targeted for imminent destruction.

> I have a force which will look down all opposition and that force is but the vanguard of a much greater. If contrary to your own interest & the just expectation of my country, you should take part in the approaching contest, you will be considered and treated as enemies and the horrors and calamities of war will stalk before you. If the barbarous … savages are let loose to murder our citizens and butcher our women and children, this war will be a war of extermination…. No white man found fighting by the side of an Indian will be taken prisoner. Instant destruction will be his lot…. The United States offer you Peace, Liberty, and Security your choice lies between these and War, Slavery, and Destruction. Choose then, but choose wisely….[3]

Hull's failure to advance with his decisive superiority of numbers was later decried as wanton cowardice by some historians, and it must be conceded that the man was strongly beset by indecision and doubts on the way to press his campaign. But beyond this he was confounded by the fact that in addition to chronic shortages of supplies and military equipment, his command was anything but unified. In fact, prior to the commencement of the invasion, several units of U.S. State militias had stood upon their constitutional and legal rights to only serve within the borders of the United States and had refused to cross the river. In addition, internecine rivalry between his junior commanders and questions of rank and privilege between the regular army and militia officers had turned Hull's force into a collection of feuding fiefdoms, incapable of sustaining a united campaign into enemy territory.

During the next two weeks, U.S. outposts and pickets along the Canard River frequently skirmished with their British counterparts, with small numbers of casualties being recorded on both sides; but, beyond a moderate probe of the British line on the Canard on July 16th, the Americans made no serious effort to advance or attack Amherstburg. Even so, the initial invasion and ongoing presence and threat of the Americans caused nearly half of the Canadian militia at Amherstburg to desert to their homes or worse, to offer a promise of refusing to do military service if the Americans attacked. However, by July 25 this ongoing lack of offensive enemy action was enough to encourage a number of Native warriors to ambush an American outpost, inflicting several casualties. Instead of causing the Americans to renew their offensive, this minor incident prompted the invaders to withdraw their outposts north and concentrate their strength at their main lines around Sandwich.

Surprised and pleased with this event, St. George recognized that he was still significantly outnumbered and outgunned and that any direct military confrontation or conflict would inevitably result in the entire destruction of his command. He therefore decided to await further developments and remain at Amherstburg. The following day, General Brock's second-in command, Colonel Henry Proctor, arrived from his previous post as senior officer on the Niagara frontier. Taking command of operations on the Detroit frontier, Proctor did not bring a significant number of additional troops or supplies, but he did bring a definite change in how future military activities were undertaken in the face of the American invasion. Reviewing the strategic and tactical situation with St. George, Proctor concurred that an all-out frontal assault on the Americans would be futile and probably catastrophic without substantial reinforcements. He therefore sent dispatches to General Brock, calling for an immediate concentration of all available regular and militia forces on the Detroit frontier and a subsequent campaign against the invaders. In the meantime, he sought to revive the morale and fighting spirit of his militias and Native allies by undertaking a show of offensive aggression. Having already learned from Hull's captured papers that the U.S. troops were short of supplies and that a large supply convoy was on its way north from the River Raisin, Proctor looked to strike at his enemy where he was weakest — behind their lines on the U.S. side of the river.

Battles of Brownston and Maguaga, August 1812

Sending across a small composite force of around one hundred regulars and militia, under the command of Captain Adam Muir (41st Regiment), Proctor looked to cut off Hull's lines of communications and possibly intercept the approaching convoy. Supporting this force were a body of Native warriors, led by Tecumseh, who initially moved south and located the expected convoy before returning and blockading the road that the convoy would have to follow. Learning of this British movement from a Canadian deserter, Hull countered by sending over two hundred Ohio State militia, commanded by Major Thomas Van Horne, with orders to link up with the convoy and escort it through to Detroit. On the morning of August 5, 1812, this relief force was marching through a section of thick woodland at the ford crossing Brownstown Creek, some fifteen miles south of Detroit. Enveloped by a thick fog, they failed to perceive their danger until it was too late when they were aggressively attacked by Tecumseh's warriors. In a matter of moments, the Americans were routed for a recorded loss of some seventeen killed and twelve wounded, while the Natives suffered only one man killed. Fleeing back to Detroit, the militiamen brought with them exaggerated tales that the British had landed large bodies of troops behind the American lines and had now cut off all communications and hope of supplies to Hull's army. A fiction, but one that was readily believed and only added to General Hull's already growing list of bad news. These items included:

- Reports that several of the Native tribes' were shifting in their attitudes from maintaining a cowed neutrality to becoming a potential or actual aggressive enemy force.
- Word that the relief column was now refusing to advance until a strong escort and guarantee of safe passage could be provided.
- News of the fall of Michilimackinac from the lips of its own garrison commander.
- An intercepted communication from the Northwest Company post at Fort William claiming (falsely or mistakenly) that there were a

potential five thousand Native warriors ready to come to the aid of the British from that quarter.

Despite these concerns, Hull continued making preparations for a major advance and assault on Amherstburg. On August 7 the final straw arrived in the form of news that General Brock was making active efforts to forward troops from Niagara and that one formation was already sailing up from Fort Erie.

In response, Hull entirely abandoned his plans for any further offensive actions. Thus, apart from a detachment of around 150 troops left behind to garrison a single fortification on the east bank, he ordered the entire evacuation of the remainder of his army from Upper Canada. During that night and following morning, a near-mutinous American army withdrew to Detroit, while Hull came under a storm of protest and criticism from his more aggressively minded regimental commanders. Seeking to re-establish his line of communications as his first priority, Hull ordered a new expedition be made by Lieutenant Colonel James Miller with over six hundred troops and two pieces of artillery. This force marched from Detroit on August 8th, passing the unburied corpses of the Brownstown rout the following day. Waiting a few miles further south, Captain Muir's far smaller force of some 150 regulars, fifty men from the Essex Embodied Militia Regiment, and two hundred Native warriors looked to repeat their earlier victory.

Late in the afternoon fighting began between the advanced pickets of both forces. This quickly escalated as the Americans pressed their advantage of numbers and used their disciplined firepower to maintain pressure on the British line, while successfully driving back the Native incursions on their flank. This was reflected on the British side by a series of tactical errors, when one flank of the British regular force mistakenly retreated instead of advancing, leaving the remainder of the line in serious danger of being outflanked and surrounded. In addition, a detachment of regular troops that had only been added to Muir's force that day mistook the Native allies for Americans and fired upon them. This precipitated a lengthy round of friendly fire between the two groups and inflicted a number of casualties upon both units. With the Americans pressing aggressively through the centre, thus splitting the British and Native force in two, the British position soon became untenable. In response, a seriously wounded Captain Muir was forced to order a retreat to the boats at the riverbank and a return to Amherstburg.

Despite having achieved a military victory at what the Americans later called the Battle of Monguagon (in British accounts, Maguaga) and successfully opened the lines of communication once more, Miller made no serious effort to press on to link up with the vital supply column. Instead, claiming the loss of most of his men's backpacks and rations to Native pilfering during the course of the fighting, he kept his force encamped at the battlefield under a succession of days of torrential rain that reduced the roadway to a quagmire of mud. Nor did things improve when Hull sent a small relief-convoy of boats — that brought only a single day's rations for Miller's men. Furthermore this flotilla of nine boats was subsequently intercepted and captured by the British during its return trip upriver, leaving Miller believing that his force could be attacked from both the front and rear. Finally, mud-caked, hungry, and exhausted, Miller's column marched back into Detroit with nothing but the moral claim of a victory to their credit, as once again the British were monitoring the southern road and the supply convoy had been told by Hull to abandon any further attempt to advance until it was provided with a suitable escort.

Thoroughly alarmed at his deteriorating situation, General Hull ordered the small detachment still remaining in Upper Canada to abandon their position on the 11th. For those Upper Canada citizens and deserting militiamen who had previously welcomed or actively assisted the invaders, their future looked dire as they were certain to be singled out for retribution by their Loyalist neighbours or even charged with treason. In consequence, while some collected their families, abandoned their homes, and fled to the U.S. east bank, others decamped into the interior of Upper Canada, to continue their opposition to the Crown as renegades and officially denounced traitors. Opposition to Hull's continued command of the U.S. "Northwest Army" now erupted in full force within his already divided command, with letters and petitions for his removal being openly circulated within the ranks and senior subordinate officers actively making plans to stage a coup.

Reacting to the Americans retreat, Proctor ordered an advance of his own smaller forces beyond the Canard River and occupied Sandwich on August 12, 1813. He then set about constructing new artillery positions at the riverbank fronting Detroit that were subsequently armed with one 18-pounder, two 12-pounders, and two 5½-inch mortars. To man these works he assigned the first of the detachments of newly arrived reinforcements sent by Brock, men from the Norfolk Militia units at Long Point under Lieutenant George Ryerson. During this same period, although isolated from the scene of action and increasingly concerned about the paucity of intelligence and information that was reaching him at York, Major-General Brock was actively pursuing a policy of preparing to meet the American invasion with force. He had already effectively ignored Prevost's previous orders on the need to act with circumspection, and now added to this by discounting a new dispatch informing him that Prevost was in the process of negotiating with General Dearborn for the implementation of an armistice.

Brock's initial plan had been to mobilize all his forces of militia and Natives and march them to Amherstburg. However, the Six Nations Native tribes on the Grand River now declared their determination to remain neutral, while several units of the militia likewise refused to come forward as ordered. With a disturbingly sparse reserve of regular troops[4] and only a half-hearted support from the provincial legislature, Brock was left with no choice but to mobilize the local Embodied Militia Regiments, who did turn out, and send what detachments he could forward to reinforce Proctor. Unfortunately, he did this without ensuring that he had the means to pay them, which greatly alarmed the army bureaucrats:

> I have this morning received a letter from Deputy General Commissary Couche, which occasions me the greatest alarm, he informs me that Major General Brock has ordered out one-third of the Militia of Upper Canada / about 4000 men / and he begs to be informed in what manner they are to be paid. The expense attending this measure will be about fifteen thousand Pounds a month, a sum which it will be impracticable to find in that country. Nor have I the means of affording effectual assistance at this moment, and if the Militia are not regularly paid, great evil will ensue, indeed, Mr. Couche represents some symptoms of discontent have already appeared.[5]

— William Robinson, Commissary General's Office to Sir George Prevost, July 30, 1812

Proroguing the Upper Canada Parliament on August 5th, Brock was encouraged to see that, heartened by the news of the capture of Michilimackinac, virtually the entire corps of the York militia had volunteered for action. However, including this force along with the regulars in an expedition to Amherstburg would leave the position at York effectively undefended. As a result, Brock only selected around one hundred men from this regiment to make the trip. He was also assisted in his plans by the arrival of two experienced senior regular officers from Lower Canada in the persons of Lieutenant Colonel Christopher Myers and Major General Roger H. Sheaffe. With these two available

**BRITISH/CANADIAN FORCES,
NIAGARA FRONTIER, JULY 2, 1812**ʸ⁴

*Fort Erie, 1st (Right) Division under
(Captain Derenzy)*

41st Regiment, 200 Rank and File
3rd Lincoln Militia, 200 Rank and File
2 x 3-pounder artillery pieces

Chippawa, 2nd Division, (Captain Bullock)

41st Regiment, 100 Rank and File
2nd Lincoln Militia, 200 Rank and File
2 x 6-pounder artillery pieces

*Queenston Heights, 3rd Division
(Captain Chambers)*

41st Regiment, 100 Rank and File
5th /6th Lincoln Militia, 200 Rank and File
2 x 3-pounder artillery pieces

Fort George, 4th (Left) Division, (Major Evans)

41st Regiment, 200 Rank and File
1st/4th Lincoln Militia, 300 Rank and File

to take over the respective commands of quartermaster general and senior commander for the Niagara frontier, Brock now felt himself free to personally advance to Amherstburg to take command of whatever situation he found upon his arrival.

AUG 5

Departing York that same day, Brock and his composite force of some forty regulars (41st Regiment) and 240 militia set out to march overland the over seventy-five miles to Port Dover. Arriving there on August 8th, Brock personally addressed a gathering of over 500 local militiamen with such dynamism that, contrary to their earlier reluctance, the men volunteered en masse to follow Brock into battle. With only sufficient vessels to transport 400, however, Brock chose to sail down the lake with whatever force could be crammed into the barely seaworthy boats, while the remainder would begin the long march along the Talbot Road. Contending with atrocious weather, rough waters, and dangerous rock shoals, the small flotilla of boats eventually landed at Amherstburg on August 13, 1812.

Reviewing the captured documents from the *Cuyahoga Packet*, Brock was able to accurately assess the growing and widespread disaffection within the American army from a stash of private letters captured at the Brownstown engagement. These came from several senior officers within Hull's corps of officers and gave clear indications of the weakness of the enemy. In response, General Brock, despite the reservations and advice of Proctor and St. George, entered into negotiations with Chief Tecumseh for a substantial counterattack on the American position at Detroit. Encouraged by Brock's aggressive stance and keen to see the Americans defeated, Tecumseh agreed to the plan.

On August 14, Brock issued a general order that firstly congratulated Proctor, St. George, and the men of the militias who had remained steadfast in the defence of their colony, while secondly expressing surprise at those of the militias who had deserted their duties. He then directed that all absentees immediately return to the colours or face the prospect of being punished according to the rules outlined in the new *Militia Act* passed earlier in the year.

Meanwhile on the American side of the river, General Hull, well aware of the growing groundswell of opposition and even the conspiracy against him, was restrained from moving against its chief plotters by the threat of it precipitating an open mutiny by the entire army. Instead, he detailed the two senior-ranking conspirators, Colonel Duncan McArthur and Colonel Lewis Cass, both of the Ohio State militia, to take a force of over 350 men and march by a circuitous inland route to link up with the supply convoy. Coincidentally, both armies began their respective operations at dawn the following day. As a result, the American's lost their most aggressive commanders and a sizeable body of troops, while the British, further reinforced by detachments that had just completed the exhausting march overland from Long Point, advanced on Sandwich. By sunset of the 15th, the American detachment was some twenty-four miles away, while the British were looking across the Detroit River as their already emplaced artillery began a bombardment of the American troop encampments at Detroit. Also during the course of that day, General Brock sent an ultimatum to Hull calling for his surrender and using a carrot and stick address to reinforce his position:

> The force at my disposal authorises me to require of you the immediate surrender of Detroit. It is far from my intention to join in a war of extermination, but you must be aware of that the numerous body of Indians who have attached themselves to my troops will be beyond control the moment the contest commences. You will find me disposed to enter into such conditions as will satisfy the most scrupulous sense of honour … that will lead to any unnecessary effusion of blood.[6]

Faced with this threat, Hull replied with a seemingly brave and defiant rebuff:

> I have received your letter of this date. I have no other reply to make, than to inform you that I am prepared to meet

any force which may be at your disposal, and any consequences which may result from any exertion of it you may think proper to make.[7]

At the same time he sent urgent orders for McArthur and Cass to immediately march back to defend Detroit, and placed his Detroit garrison on full alert for an imminent British attack. Before dawn on August 16, 1812, six hundred of Brock's Native allies crossed the Detroit River and landed at Spring Wells, three miles south of Detroit, to secure a landing ground. Shortly thereafter, a flotilla of small boats containing Brock's main force of some 330 regulars, 400 militia, and five cannon made their own crossing, all under the protective screen of ships from the Provincial Marine department.[*8] Seeking to further magnify the apparent strength of his small invasion force, Brock had previously directed that as many of the militia as possible were to be issued cast-off or spare regular redcoat uniforms to make them look like "real" soldiers to the Americans. Landing unopposed and forming their column-of-march, Brock received intelligence that some of McArthur and Cass's troops were only three miles to his south. Faced with the prospect of being caught in a vice between two enemy forces, Brock would have been entirely justified in retreating back to the east side of the river; instead he ordered an immediate advance

BRITISH FORCES LISTED AS ELIGIBLE TO CLAIM PRIZE MONEY RESULTING FROM THEIR INVOLVEMENT IN THE SURRENDER AT DETROIT, AUGUST 16, 1812[*8]

General and Staff: 15 Officers, 3 Other Ranks
Royal Artillery: 1 Officer, 29 Other Ranks
41st Regiment: 13 Officers, 289 Other Ranks
Royal Newfoundland Fencible Regiment: 4 Officers, 49 Other Ranks
1st/3rd York Militia: 6 Officers, 105 Other Ranks
2nd York/5th Lincoln Militia: 3 Officers, 62 Other Ranks
2nd Norfolk/1st Middlesex Militia Regiments: 7 Officers, 62 Other Ranks
Oxford Militia: 13 Other Ranks
1st Essex Militia: 22 Officers, 290 Other Ranks
2nd Essex Militia: 23 Officers, 144 Other Ranks
1st Kent Militia: 9 Officers, 54 Other Ranks
Indian Department: 1 Officer, 5 Other Ranks
Unassigned: 3 Officers, 1 Other Ranks
Total: 117 Officers, 1243 Other Ranks

upon Detroit. Awaiting his just-over-a-thousand troops and Native warriors were Hull's garrison of an estimated 2,500 American troops, entrenched behind a line of strong earthworks and fortifications, bristling with no less than thirty-three cannon.

Advancing to within a mile of the fortifications, Brock halted the column and began to deploy his line. In a deft example of bravado and sleight of hand, the general spread out his units to make them

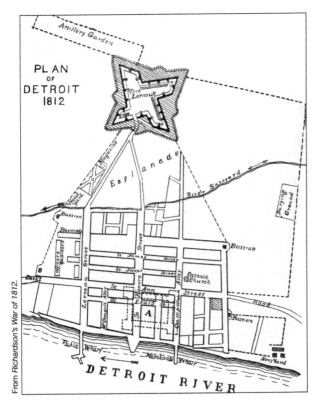

From Richardson's War of 1812.

PLAN
OF
DETROIT
1812

The plan of the town and fortifications at Detroit in 1812.

to the point where sizeable numbers of militia began abandoning their assigned posts for the sanctuary of the distant forests. Seeing his force dwindling, and already visibly shaken by the effect of the British bombardment, Hull was beset by the dilemma that as well as being the military commander of the garrison, he was also the governor of Michigan, making the welfare and safety of the civilian populace his direct responsibility. If he gave battle and lost, Brock's Native warriors could well be unleashed,

AMERICAN TROOPS SURRENDERED AT DETROIT, AUGUST 16, 1812[9]

(N.B. Not including subsequent surrenders of detached U.S. forces)

Regulars

Cavalry (2 Troops)
Artillery (1 Company)
Infantry: Fourth Regiment

Militias

First United States Volunteers Regiment (Detachment)
Third United States Volunteers Regiment (Detachment)
Third Ohio State Militia Regiment
First Michigan Territory Militia Regiment

Estimated total: 2,500 All Ranks

appear more numerous. In addition, he made extensive use of the Natives to engage in psychological warfare by making probes and threatening attacks on the American flanks. By these ruses, and supported by the continued cannonade from his batteries on the east bank of the Detroit River, Brock succeeded in demoralizing General Hull and his army with terrifying consequences for all the Americans in Detroit. Making his decision, Hull gave the order for his troops to hold their fire while he entered into negotiations for a formal capitulation. Following a brief exchange of demands, General Hull not only agreed to surrender the fort, its garrison, and all supplies therein,[9],[10] but also the relief column at Frenchtown on the River Raisin, the garrison at the Maumee Rapids, and the forces of McArthur and Cass — who were now conspicuous by their continued absence. In fact, these latter officers had previously deliberately ignored Hull's orders to return when the threat was initially revealed on the 14th, and remained encamped overnight before making a more leisurely return march until they came within two miles of the fort and heard the sounds of the British cannonade from across the river. Without making any reconnaissance or notifying Hull of their presence, they ordered their troops to turn about once again and made a hasty retreat to the River Rouge, where they remained until officially notified that Detroit had been surrendered. Whereupon the two officers made a vehement public show of being outraged and surprised at Hull's capitulation, and condemned him for sending them from Detroit at a time of danger. By this they successfully established their own alibis and distanced themselves from the inevitable official American censure that would follow, once news of the surrender became public.

ORDNANCE, WEAPONS, AND SUPPLIES CAPTURED AT DETROIT, AUGUST 16, 1812[10]

Guns
Iron: 9 x 24-pounders plus 5 Garrison carriages and 2 Field carriages
8 x 12-pounders plus 5 Garrison carriages
5 x 9-pounders plus 4 Garrison carriages
3 x 6-pounders plus 3 Garrison carriages and 3 Field carriages
Brass: 3 x 6-pounders
2 x 4-pounders plus 2 Field carriages
1 x 3-pounder plus 2 Field carriages
1 x 8" Howitzer, plus 1 Field carriage
1 x 5" Howitzer, plus 1 Field carriage
1 Field carriage for a 2 ¾" Howitzer
Artillery Shot: (cumulative totals for all of the above calibres)
10,908 Solid Round Shot
226 Grape Shot rounds
265 Case (Cannister) Shot rounds
4,391 Explosive Shells
2,500 Muskets
2,500 Bayonets
2,500 Cartouche Boxes with belts
500 Rifles
39,000 Flints
80,000 Prepared Musket Cartridges
10 Hundredweight (.55 tonne) of loose musket balls
1 Ton (1.1 tonnes) of loose Buckshot

In addition to these logistical and troop surrenders, in the aftermath of the surrender, General Brock's proclamation to the populace of the Michigan Territory (August 16, 1812), stipulated a claim that was to have significant repercussions upon the future conduct and course of the war. Namely that the territory had been ceded to the control and authority of the British Crown, and therefore was now de facto part of British North America and Upper Canada.

> Whereas the territory of Michigan was this day by Capitulation ceded to the Arms of His Britannick Majesty, without any other condition than the protection of private property, and wishing to give an early proof of the moderation and Justice of His Majesty's Government, I do hereby announce to all the Inhabitants of the said Territory that the Laws heretofore in existence shall continue in force until His Majesty's pleasure be known ...[11]

Interestingly, in most of the subsequent American histories on the war, this territorial loss of part of the United States is either entirely ignored or dismissed as merely British wordplay or bravado. However, in the light of the following details, there can be little doubt that as far as Brock and his administration was concerned this change in allegiance and control was real enough.

- The territory had previously been British property and had only been handed over to American control eighteen years previous as part of the treaty's dealing with the American Revolution. In addition, many of its inhabitants were previously British subjects, a status Britain maintained was a permanent fact and not revocable.

- On August 21, Proctor issued a subsequent proclamation of his own, stating:

> Whereas the Territory of Michigan, was on the sixteenth day of August, one thousand eight hundred twelve, Ceded by Capitulation to the arms of HIS BRITANNIC MAJESTY, & the American flag was removed and the British flag substituted ... be it known, that I, the undersigned, HENRY PROCTOR, Colonel in the Military forces of HIS BRITANNIC MAJESTY, now Commanding in the Territory of Michigan, do make & establish ... the following Regulations for the civil administration of the said Territory ...[12]

- Several letters were subsequently exchanged between Colonel Proctor and American Chief Justice of the Territory Augustus Woodward, over defining the area the British now officially controlled and other details of the change in the existing American administration to British hands. In these communications, both officials refer to the "change of flag" and the territory being "ceded."

- Governor Hull never denounced or repudiated the validity of the British claim.
- In the following months, Proctor established a new bureaucracy of civil administration, and Michigan citizens were called upon to swear the oath of allegiance to the British Crown or quit the territory — while many chose to take the oath, many others refused and left.
- Lands on the west side of the Detroit River were officially deeded over as settlements to Native allies by Proctor on behalf of the British Government.

Furthermore, when the news of the "ceding" reached Washington, far from being simply dismissed or denounced as invalid, it was considered such a political disaster that it almost toppled the administration. The War Hawks saw the ceding as a stain upon the national pride of the United States, requiring an immediate and total commitment on the part of the nation to reclaim its lost lands as soon as possible, again countering the subsequent claims that it was merely an error in British phrasing.

In the immediate term, the American "Northwestern Army" was effectively eliminated and the biggest problem facing Brock was what to do with his overwhelming number of prisoners. After leaving behind the sick and wounded (117 Officers, 480 Other Ranks), the remaining regular officers and their troops (532 All Ranks), plus a large proportion of militia officers and men (1034 All Ranks), were transported to either Lower Canada (regulars) or the Niagara frontier (militias).[13] For those now in Lower Canada, they were destined to either remain as prisoners of war for the duration of the conflict or, in the case of the more lucky individuals, repatriated to the United States on the condition of having given their "paroles." This nicety of warfare in an age of "gentlemen" required individuals to sign an oath not to engage in any further combat or offensive activities until formally and officially released from their parole by a *mutually agreed* and signed written declaration issued by *both* of the warring governments. Alternatively, the parole could be ended if they were officially and *mutually* exchanged for an equal number of British and Canadian equivalent ranks then being held as prisoners in the U.S. This parole system was also adopted for both the American militias taken to the Niagara frontier and those left behind on the Detroit frontier, allowing the men to eventually return to their homes.

Buoyed by his stunning and unexpected victory, Brock was also anxious to return to the Niagara frontier as soon as possible. Having previously dispatched the *Queen Charlotte* with her cargo of 130 American regular prisoners of war for Fort Erie, he followed on August 19 in the smaller *Cuyahoga Packet*, now renamed the *Chippawa*, crammed with around twenty regular troops under the guard of a handful of the York Militia. During the passage, the disgruntled prisoners were seen as such a threat to the vessel that the ship's captain was forced to order their confinement below decks, while their guards were equally forced to remain exposed on deck during a series of severe thunderstorms that threatened to swamp the ship. Approaching Fort Erie on the night of the 22–23rd, the vessel was becalmed in a dense fog bank and anchored to await the dawn. With daylight, to the British commander's consternation he found that the *Chippawa* had moored within rifle-shot range of the American shoreline off the village of Buffalo. Seeing what they still believed to be an American vessel, curious citizens began to gather along the shore to hear news from the Detroit frontier. Under imminent threat of being challenged, discovered, boarded, and captured, Brock and the other identifiable "redcoats" were forced to remain hidden, while the boat's crew attempted to tow the ship away from the shore using a small longboat. However, despite strenuous efforts, the current of the Niagara River prevented the boat making any appreciable movement upstream. Unable to escape under their own efforts, Brock took a chance and authorized one of the militiamen to fire off a single shot in an attempt to attract the attention of the *Queen Charlotte* moored across the channel off Fort Erie, without drawing the suspicions of the nearer Americans on shore. Fortunately, the attempt worked and the *Queen Charlotte* came across to investigate, protecting the smaller vessel with her battery of guns while providing additional towing help that allowed the *Chippawa* to draw away from the American shore and moor off Fort Erie. Collecting those prisoners already landed, Brock marched them along the river road, in plain sight of the gathering American forces on the east bank, possibly as a warning of their potential fate if they too attempted an invasion. A message that obviously carried some weight if the contents of a letter from Major General Van Rensselaer to Major General Dearborn, dated September 1, 1812, is to be considered accurate:

> … it is a fact that cannot be concealed that the surrender of General Hull's army has spread great alarm among the inhabitants of this Frontier, and I every day perceive strong symptoms of distrust among the troops. They have seen their countrymen surrendered without a single effort, and marched, prisoners, before their eyes. They cannot comprehend it.[14]

CHAPTER 4

Actions Along the St. Lawrence River, July to December 1812

At the eastern end of Upper Canada, following the initial foray against the small American flotilla at the outset of the war, the St. Lawrence frontier settled down to a state of relative calm as both sides sought to avoid "rocking the boat" and thereby triggering reprisals. From the British point of view, this was a practical necessity, as the river constituted their main lifeline of supplies and reinforcements up to Kingston, York, and the Niagara and Detroit frontiers. Equally, the residents on the American side had practical reasons for maintaining the peace. Most of the population were Federalist (anti-war) and many farmers and businessmen had lucrative dealings with the British commissariat department on the other side of the river that they were keen not to jeopardize. One prime example of this co-operative, non-belligerent attitude can be seen in the following case. A small flotilla of American boats had been returning upriver to Ogdensburg from Montreal in June, laden with a cargo of merchandise, when news of the declaration of war reached Cornwall. The boats were immediately impounded under the orders of the local garrison's commanding officer, as enemy goods that were to be seized and sold by the Crown. However, within a matter of days, private negotiations between the interested parties at Prescott and Ogdensburg resulted in a petition being forwarded to General Brock from fourteen of Prescott's leading citizens, including several who were officers in the Embodied Militias. In this petition the argument was made that as the goods in question were private property, and not military supplies, and the vital commissariat trade with Ogdensburg might

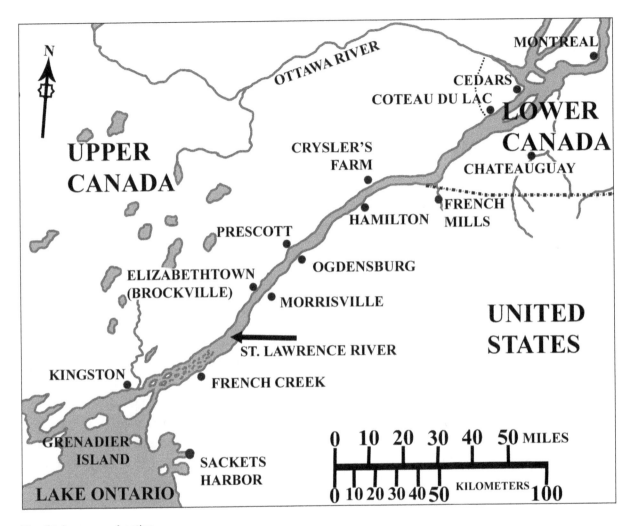

The St. Lawrence frontier.

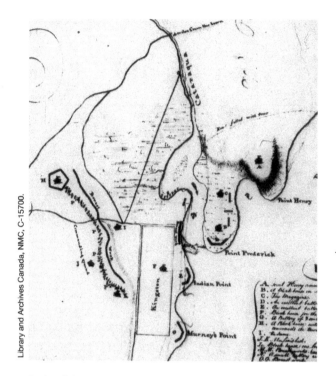

A detail from a contemporary map of the defences constructed during the war to protect the vital supply depot and shipbuilding centre of Kingston.

suffer if the capture and sale was allowed to stand, that it was in the best interests of the British war effort to let the vessels and their cargo go. General Brock concurred and the vessels were released.[1]

On the other hand, the potential threat level rose later in the month when the New York State militia officer, Brigadier General Jacob Brown, was

sent to Ogdensburg with a detachment of troops and orders to shut down the British river traffic.

An initial attempt by Brown to mount a raid across the river, to capture the British armed schooner *Duke of Gloucester*, was planned for the night of July 22–23. However, although the boats were prepared, the call for militia volunteers fell flat, with only sixty-six of the requested 120 men stepping forward, forcing Brown to cancel the operation.[2]

On July 30, the American armed schooner *Julia* and a large gunboat, sailing out of Sackets Harbor, appeared upriver and proceeded to engage the *Duke of Gloucester* and another Provincial Marine vessel, the *Earl of Moria*, that were docked at Prescott. After an inconclusive engagement the two sides disengaged, and while the British ships sailed west, to Kingston, the *Julia* and the gunboat joined the vessels trapped at Ogdensburg.

Little occurred during the month of August, as news arrived from Quebec City that an armistice was to be imposed. This came about following word that the British government had repealed its contentious Orders-in-Council affecting American maritime trading rights with Britain's wartime enemy, France. Because these issues were cited by the American government as the principal reason and cause of the war being declared, Sir George Provost had written to Major General Henry

Kingston, Sir E.W. Grier, artist, circa 1896 (after Admiral Henry Bayfield R.N.). A view of the shipyards at Point Frederick (centre) and the town of Kingston (right distant), as it looked at the end of the war from the hillside alongside Fort Henry (left).

Kingston, 1815, E.E. Vidal, artist, 1815. This image is a detail taken from a larger painting showing Fort Henry as the Americans would have seen it from their ships.

Watercolours (artist not known) depicting two of many varieties of gunboat used during the War of 1812, showing how the combination of both sail and oar were required for manoeuvering through the narrow channels and swift currents of the St. Lawrence River near Kingston and the Thousand Islands region.

Dearborn, recommending an armistice until the U.S. government's position on settling the outstanding issues between the two governments was known. An unofficial regional suspension of hostilities was therefore established. However, this armistice was subsequently rejected by President James Madison and Secretary of War William Eustis, who ordered a recommencement of hostilities to conquer Canada. From the British perspective, while the armistice had resulted in the withdrawal of most of the enemy's troops from Ogdensburg, it had also seen the unimpeded release of the trapped vessels, which now made their way upriver to Lake Ontario and Sackets Harbor, becoming valuable

additions to the American naval flotilla being assembled at that port.

The following month, matters started to heat up once again once the official declaration of the ending of the armistice took effect on September 4, 1812.

THE BATTLE OF MATILDA, SEPTEMBER 16, 1812

On September 16, a flotilla of thirty-three heavily laden bateaux and boats were in the process of sailing for Kingston with a cargo of supplies and passengers, composed principally of the dependents of

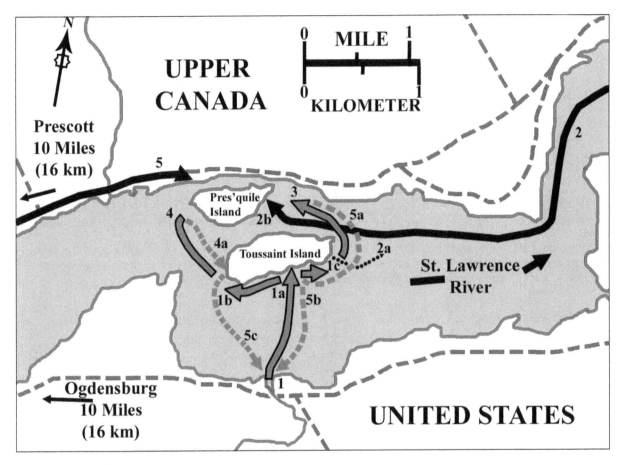

The Battle of Matilda (September 16, 1812).

men from the Royal Newfoundland Regiment who had been previously dispatched to Kingston. They had almost reached Prescott when an attempt was made by the Americans to capture the vessels. Led by a strong detachment of troops,[*4] the Americans landed on the small mid-river Toussaint Island,(near present-day Cardinal) after dark on the 15th and took the resident Toussaint family prisoner. They

The Battle of Matilda (September 16, 1812).

1. U.S. forces (1) sail to Toussaint Island and land troops, who imprison the Toussaint family and then establish an ambush position along the shoreline. Two gunboats (1a) move upriver (1b), while the Durham boat moves downriver (1c) to take up their respective ambush positions.

2. The British convoy flotilla (2) sails up the river, maintaining their proximity to the Canadian shoreline. Approaching Toussaint Island, the American Durham boat is spotted and the convoy halts. Mr. Toussaint escapes the American custody and paddles to warn the convoy (2a). The convoy changes course and heads toward Presqu'ile Island, where they ground offshore in the shallow water (2b). The passengers and crews evacuate the boats and take cover on the island.

3. The American Durham boat pursues the British flotilla and opens fire on the evacuees (3) as the American land forces fire from Toussaint Island.

4. The American gunboats move out from hiding (4), intending to land troops on Presqu'ile Island, but are driven off by fire from the defenders and return to Toussaint Island (4a), losing in the process one boat that drifts away downstream.

5. Local Canadian militias, alerted to the ambush and engagement arrive (5) and engage the Americans. The Americans break off the attack (5a) and retire to their remaining boats, to be evacuated back to the U.S. side of the river (5b) (5c).

then set up their ambush positions on land, while the boats remained hidden, ready to strike once the trap had been sprung.

At dawn the following morning, the British flotilla was approaching the position but received a timely warning from Mr. Toussaint, who had escaped to his canoe and, while under fire from the Americans, paddled downriver to deliver his warning.

In response, the flotilla immediately changed course and headed toward the small island of Presqu'ile, to the north of Toussaint Island, only to come under a heavy fire from the Americans. Interestingly, a passenger aboard the British boats,

TROOPS INVOLVED AT THE OUTSET OF THE BATTLE OF MATILDA, SEPTEMBER 16, 1812[4]

American

1 Gunboat (Adjutant Daniel Church), 18 crew
2 Durham boats (Captain Griffin), 70 crew
Volunteer militia (Major Nash)
estimated 200–250 All Ranks

British (Major Heathcote)

33 bateaux and longboats
Royal Newfoundland Regiment (crews)
49th Regiment
10th Royal Veterans Battalion
Dundas Militia
estimated total 138 All Ranks

Patrick Finan (the son of the Royal Newfoundland's regimental quartermaster), documented this event, showing that even in the midst of combat and the face of death, humour can sometimes be found:

We had proceeded up the river … when within a short distance of a narrow passage between an island and the mainland through which we must pass, one of the Captains of the regiment, who was in the foremost batteau, imagined he saw something like a Durham boat … this being a rather suspicious circumstance, he ordered the men to cease from rowing.… While waiting for the other bateaux to come up, a Canadian was observed in a canoe … paddling with all his might and crying to us that there were Americans on the island. This confirmed the suspicions; and the boats were ordered to the shore … but when about twenty yards from the edge of the water, the boats grounded and could be brought no nearer.…

The balls were flying about us, perforating the sides of the boats, dropping into the water in every direction and threatening immediate destruction to all on board, great confusion prevailed; and as soon as it was observed that the boats could not advance to the shore, our only alternative was to leap into the water and make the best of our way to it.… As our boat was at the upper end of the division, I had a full view of the whole detachment;

… men, women, and children … some up to their knees in water, some driving it before them like ships in full sail; others dashing in and making it fly about them on all sides; women screaming, children bawling, officers commanding; but all endeavouring to get out of the reach of the shot as fast as possible.…

There was … a lady, wife of an officer in Kingston … and as she had been in a delicate state of health for some time [translation: approaching the end of her pregnancy] she was unwilling, notwithstanding the imminent danger that surrounded her, to venture into the water if she could possibly avoid it. While hesitating, an officer in the next boat, observing her situation, came to her and requested her to get on his back, in order that he might carry her to the land, which she gladly consented to.

They were both particularly stout, bulky people; and they had not proceeded far until the officer, owing to his heavy burden, sank so deep in the soft mud, that he actually stuck fast, and could not move a step father....[5]

Unable to extricate himself, the officer was forced to apologetically notify his passenger that he had no option but to ask her to step down, which she reluctantly did. Patrick Finian continued:

If the reader can fancy to himself a great fat fellow, in a long red coat and cocked hat, up to his knees in water and leading by the hand, very cordially, but in a great hurry, as fat a lady with flowing garments ... sometimes moving on pretty well, at others rather puzzled to get their feet extricated from the mud, and all the while in terrible dread of being shot....[6]

Fortunately the duo, and the remainder of the passengers, all reached land safely. However, during the confusion of this impromptu landing, the American gunboat joined the engagement, firing roundshot and grape toward the troops and civilians alike as they scrambled off the beach and sought cover amongst the island's trees.

After some ineffectual exchanges of fire between the two islands, the Americans attempted to outflank the British position by sending over the gunboats loaded with a detachment of twenty men led by Lieutenant Goss. In response, Lieutenant Duncan Clark (1st Dundas Militia) led a similar detachment across the island and

immediately fired on them with such effect that they retreated back to Tusaut's island, a distance of about 100 yards, where they landed and took shelter in the woods, with the loss of one of their boats ... which was taken possession of after drifting down the river by a party of the militia....[7]

Neither side could effectively outmanoeuvre or attack the other, and thus the two groups remained in stalemate on the two islands, exchanging shots as targets of opportunity occurred. At the same time, increasing numbers of detachments from the alerted Canadian Militia on the north bank of the river were arriving, increasing the British firing lines:

Captain Ault and Lieutenant Dorin were soon on the field of action with the remainder of the Company, as well as Captain Shaw with the men of the neighbourhood and in a short time, the people of Matilda and many from Williamsburg assembled on Presq'uile Island with

Colonel MacDonell commanding the Dundas Militia at the time.

Such was the anxiety of the people to meet their old enemy, the Rebels of "76" that aged ... veterans who had served under Sir William and Sir Johnson were foremost in the fight....[8]

This force was further enhanced by the arrival of two companies of the 1st Grenville Militia (Captains Hugh Munroe and Philip Dulmage) as well as a 9-pounder cannon under Lieutenant Richard Fraser (2nd Grenville), "whose well directed shots, together with the fire of musketry kept up by the Dundas Militia, compelled the Americans to retire from their position on Tusait's Island and make a precipitate retreat to their own side of the St. Lawrence...."[9]

Faced with the prospect of fighting around newly arrived 300 militia infantry, plus artillery, as well as the original detachments from the boats, the Americans quickly broke off the engagement and used their gunboat and surviving Durham boat to ferry their troops back to their own side of the river. No clear account or record of the casualties from this engagement is known to exist, but it appears to have been less than half a dozen killed and wounded for either side.

The final event during the month took place on September 21, when party of around ninety-five U.S. troops, drawn from the First U.S. Rifle Regiment (led by Captain Benjamin Forsyth) and supported by a detachment of around thirty-four volunteer militia (under Captain Samuel McNitt), made a sortie on Gananoque, just to the east of Kingston. Sailing up from Sackets Harbor, the American's were detected by militia cavalry pickets as they landed around two miles (3.2 kilometres) from the village. Upon their arrival, the Americans found themselves facing an alerted but motley collection of barely trained and poorly armed local militia from the Leeds County Embodied Militia Regiment, dressed in worn-out and cast-off redcoats acquired from Kingston. Believing they were facing regular troops, Forsyth's men formed line and engaged the defenders. Following a short exchange of gunfire that inflicted around a dozen casualties among the Canadian militiamen, the American regulars advanced and quickly brushed aside the defender's token resistance. They then occupied the village and ransacked the militia warehouse before burning the building and its contents of over 150 barrels of provisions. They then returned to Sackets Harbor with a haul of twelve prisoners, forty-one muskets, and three barrels of prepared ammunition.[10]

Tensions mounted once again in October, when troops led by General Brown and Captain Forsyth arrived at Ogdensburg, this time to stay. As he had done previously, Brown attempted to cut off the

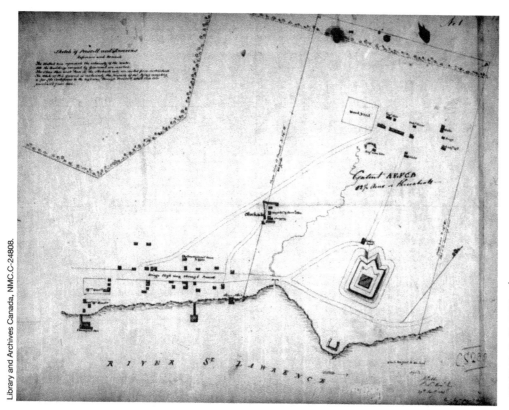

The British garrison post at Prescott, the first (easternmost) real defensive fortification on the St. Lawrence River in Upper Canada.

British line of communication and transport by firing his artillery at any British vessel that came in sight.

In response, the garrison at Prescott, under Colonel Robert Lethbridge, attempted to mount an attack against Ogdensburg on Sunday, October 4, 1812. Commencing with an artillery bombardment, some thirty boats, loaded with around 150 Canadian Fencible troops from the Glengarry Light Infantry Regiment and 600 militiamen drawn from the Leeds, Stormont, and Dundas Embodied Militia regiments, set out to land and capture Ogdensburg. As they approached the American shore, however, they came under an increasing level of American artillery and then musket fire from around 1,200 troops, which included Brown and Forsyth's new arrivals, supported by detachments of local militia.

A view from the 1813 earthen ramparts of Fort Wellington at Prescott. The existing central blockhouse is a postwar construction. The far bank, beyond the St. Lawrence River, is the United States.

In response, with their vessels being damaged and taking casualties amongst the tightly packed men, one boat after another abandoned the crossing. As a result, the entire flotilla attack collapsed, to the humiliation of the British and the added prestige of the American military commanders. From that point onward, the American presence at Ogdensburg was seen as a growing threat. Within weeks additional companies of riflemen, as well as three companies of artillerymen with three guns, had augmented the American garrison. On the British side of the river, the failure of the expedition led to the rapid replacement of the aging Colonel Lethbridge as Prescott's garrison commander by a far more experienced combat officer, Lieutenant Colonel Thomas Pearson (23rd Regiment). Under Pearson's demanding and expert hand, the previously lethargic men of the regular forces were soon drilled into a better fighting efficiency, and the militias started a course of instruction to enable them to fight with better coordination and discipline alongside the regulars. Pearson also made detailed plans for the attack and destruction of Ogdensburg. Unfortunately, Prevost's directives for maintaining a non-aggressive posture left Pearson and his now-ready troops frustrated, to say the least, as 1812 drew to a close.

CHAPTER 5

Threats and Counter-Threats Along the Niagara River,
July to October 1812

According to Secretary of War Eustis's original plan to conquer the Canadas, diversionary attacks upon the Detroit and Niagara frontiers would draw British reserves away from Montreal and Quebec, thus allowing the main American thrust to enter Lower Canada through Vermont against reduced opposition. In reality, the failure of government recruiters to raise any significant military units in New England, coupled with the debacle of General Hull at Detroit, effectively derailed the 1812 American war effort. Desperate to create some kind of military success, the administration pressured General Dearborn to produce positive results on the Niagara front to counter their failures elsewhere. For Dearborn, this came as an unwelcome surprise, for he was hardly aware that the Niagara region came under his jurisdiction,

while the quality of the region's commanders had hardly risen to the challenge of the moment. In fact, although it had only been a month since war had been declared, the troops on the Niagara frontier had already been under the command of both Brigadier General William Wadsworth and Major General Amos Hall. On July 13, 1812, they gained their third new commander in the person of Major General Stephen Van Rensselaer.

A member of an influential New York State family, Van Rensselaer had been politically opposed to the prospect of war, but had been manoeuvred into accepting command of the "Army of the Centre" by his political opponent, the incumbent governor, Daniel D. Tompkins. For Tompkins, this seemingly contradictory act actually held political merit, for although a military victory would

General Stephen Van Rensselaer, artist unknown. Manipulated into a command he did not want, he later became the scapegoat for the American defeat at Queenston.

New York State Governor, Daniel D. Tompkins. Political opponent of General Stephen Van Rensselaer, he used the general's defeat at Queenston to win re-election.

bring Van Rensselaer fame and honour, declining the post would brand him as failing to support his country in time of war. Furthermore, accepting the post would handicap Van Rensselaer's ability to mount a political campaign against Tompkins, and any military defeat would seal Van Rensselaer's political fate entirely.

During the remainder of the summer, once he saw the task before him, Van Rensselaer was in a constant state of alarm that Brock would take the initiative and attack across the Niagara River, a circumstance for which he believed there was no effective defence:

> Sir ... At this hour I have received no reinforcements of men, no supplies of ordnance, tents nor ammunition. There are not ten rounds per man on the Niagara frontier, nor have we lead to make cartridges. We are extremely deficient of medicine and hospital stores; of lint and bandage cloth we have none, nor any surgical instruments.... The company lately under the command of Captain Jennings in Lieutenant Col. Swift's regiment had become so clamorous for pay, and contended so strenuously that their time had expired, that I have ordered them to be dismissed.[1]

— Major General Van Rensselaer to Major General Dearborn, September 1, 1812

Under these circumstances, orders that had previously been issued to the various posts not to stir up any unnecessary trouble were reissued, a command that at least one detachment of over-enthusiastic young volunteers serving at the newly constructed Fort Tompkins, near Black Rock,

found themselves unable to obey, with inevitable consequences.

> I commanded the gun that threw the first ball at the enemy [on August 13, 1812] ... until now we had not been permitted by our superiors to get up any quarrel with our neighbours, and were not allowed to fire a gun except with blank cartridges for the purpose of practice, and we were tired of lounging and doing nothing. So accordingly the British came near the river and commenced building a battery with some 30 or 40 men. Now the question was, should we permit them to do it? We could do nothing unless slyly done, orders being against us. However, it seemed most too much to allow our enemies to erect machines immediately under our noses to kill us with. We accordingly consulted as to whether we were able to get a ball to the gun unknown to our officers.... After waiting for a favourable opportunity, the ball went in, unknown to any except those engaged in it. Our next business was to gauge the range with the view to have the ball fall short of them, as we did not desire to kill them, but merely to drive them away. All

things being ready, the match was applied, BANG! went the gun. The ball struck where we intended. The British were so completely enveloped in smoke and dust that not one of them could be seen, but as soon as they could be, we found them running in every direction.... To complete the mortification on their part, we took off our chapeaux and gave them three cheers. When our officers made inquiries who had disobeyed orders, no one knew anything about it. They did not try very hard to find out.... Now as each party was waiting for the other, the restraint was removed. The next morning, the British opened upon us with long guns. The balls that went over our battery would take out our barracks, which were in the rear.

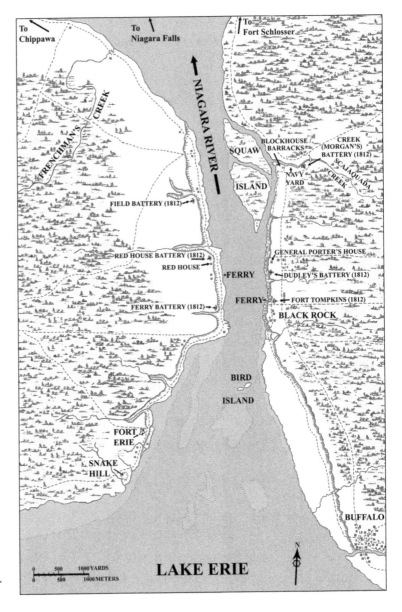

The upper (southern) end of the Niagara River as it flows out from Lake Erie and the various military positions established in 1812.

They were built of poles, and before night not one pole was left upon the other....[2]

— Lieutenant Archer Galloway, New York Militia Artillery

Fortunately for the Americans, Prevost's directives on maintaining a defensive posture, the temporary armistice, and the limited number of troops at his disposal compelled Brock to remain on his own side of the river, thus giving Van Rensselaer time to receive substantial reinforcements.[*3] Upon arrival, however, these new units found the local command structure in a shambles, as were the arrangements for accommodations, supplies of food, ammunition, weapons, and almost every other necessity of campaign life. As a result, increased levels of insubordination and dissatisfaction led to desertions and outbreaks of mutiny within the various regiments.

Nor were things better at the top of the command structure as Quartermaster General Peter B. Porter and the local representative of the governor, Nicholas Gray, (both of whom were War Hawks and held political and personal animosity toward Van Rensselaer) repeatedly sought to undermine his authority. This schism was further widened when Brigadier General Alexander Smyth arrived at Buffalo in late September, with over 1,600 regular

Brigadier General Alexander Smyth, the self-proclaimed military "expert" who made considerable contributions to the failures experienced by the American military on the Niagara frontier in 1812.

troops. Technically, Smyth was under the command of Van Rensselaer, and should have reported his arrival in person to his commanding officer. Instead, Smyth's ego refused to acknowledge the authority of a militiaman over a regular and he defiantly set up a rival command headquarters of his own at Buffalo.

I had intended to have reported myself personally; but the conclusions I have

AMERICAN FORCES, NIAGARA FRONTIER, OCTOBER 1812[*3]

Fort Niagara (Lieutenant Colonel Fenwick)

First Artillery Regiment (Captain Nathan Leonard), 115 All Ranks

Sixth Regiment (Captain John McChesney), 500 All Ranks

Twenty-third Regiment (Major James R. Mullany), 300 All Ranks

Four Mile Creek

Thirteenth Regiment (Lieutenant Colonel John Chrystie), 400 All Ranks

Lewiston (Brigadier General Wadsworth)

Eighteenth New York Militia (Lieutenant Colonel Hugh Dobbin), 500 All Ranks

Nineteenth New York Militia (Lieutenant Colonel Henry Bloom), 500 All Ranks

Twentieth New York Militia (Lieutenant Colonel Peter Allen), 500 All Ranks

Independent Company of New York Militia Light Dragoons (Captain Allen), unknown number

Militia Rifle "Battalion" (Major Charles Mosely), 100 All Ranks

Fort Schlosser and Falls of Niagara

Second Artillery Regiment (Lieutenant Colonel Winfield Scott), 100 All Ranks

Sixteenth New York Militia (Lieutenant Colonel Farrand Stranahan), 500 All Ranks

Seventeenth New York Militia (Lieutenant Colonel Thompson Mead), 500 All Ranks

Black Rock and Buffalo (Brigadier General Smyth)

Fifth Regiment (Colonel Homer Milton), unknown number

Twelfth Regiment (Colonel Thomas Parker), unknown number

Thirteenth Regiment, (Colonel Peter Schuyler), unknown number

Fourteenth Regiment (Colonel William H. Winder), 337 All Ranks

(Total of 1,300 All Ranks)

Swift's Volunteer Regiment (Lieutenant Colonel Philetus Swift), 501 All Ranks

Hopkin's Volunteer Regiment (Lieutenant Colonel Silas Hopkins), 200 All Ranks

Pennsylvania Volunteer Militia Regiment (Captain Allison), 50 Rank and File

(Captain Collins) 62 Rank and File

(Captain Philips) 45 Rank and File

drawn as to the interests of the service have determined me to stop at this place for the present … I am of the opinion that our crossing should be effected between Fort Erie and Chippawa. It has therefore seemed to me proper to encamp the U.S. troops near Buffalo, there to prepare for offensive operations.[4]

— Brigadier General Smyth to Major General Van Renssalaer, Buffalo, September 29, 1812

In the days that followed, Smyth repeatedly ignored Van Rensselaer's calls for a conference with the other military commanders so as to decide how the campaign would be prosecuted, citing as his justification the superiority of his own judgement as to where the proposed invasion should occur. Nor was Van Rensselaer receiving any support from General Dearborn, who wrote several communications stressing the political expectations of Washington for a victory, while at the same time leaving no doubt that additional military assistance could not be expected in the near future. He also added the codicil that in the event of a British attack, Van Rensselaer should "be prepared to make good a secure retreat as the last resort."[5] Little wonder then that Van Rensselaer replied with the following communication less than a week before the planned attack:

> Our best troops are raw: many of them dejected by the distress their families suffer by their absence, and many have not necessary clothing.… The blow must be struck soon or all the toil and expense of the campaign will go for nothing; or worse than nothing, for the whole will be tinged with dishonour. With my present force it would be rash to attempt an offensive operation.…[6]

Whether he thought an attack was rash or not, however, Van Rensselaer was left with little alternative but to continue planning his offensive and put on a brave face to his troops and commander. His initial plan was to

> … immediately concentrate the regular force in the neighbourhood of Niagara, and the militia here; make the best possible dispositions, and, at the same time that the regulars shall pass from the Four Mile Creek to a point in the rear of Fort George, and take it by storm; I will pass the river here [Lewiston] and carry the heights of Queenston. Should we

succeed, we shall effect a great discomfiture of the enemy, by breaking their line of communication, driving their shipping from the mouth of the river, leaving them no rallying point in this part of the country, appalling the minds of the Canadians, and opening a wide and safe communication for our supplies....[7]

However, this plan never progressed beyond the proposal stage as Smyth's continued insubordinate attitude and refusal to submit to Van Rensselaer's authority effectively restricted the planned expedition to that segment proposed for Queenston.

As the days passed, pressure mounted on Van Rensselaer, especially when news arrived from Buffalo of a small but significant American military success made on the night of October 8–9 by the capture of two British brigs, the *Detroit* (formerly the *Adams*, captured from the Americans at Detroit) and the *Caledonia*, both of which had just moored off Fort Erie, laden with weapons and prisoners from Brock's victory at Detroit. The American boarding parties consisted of a combined force of regular soldiers

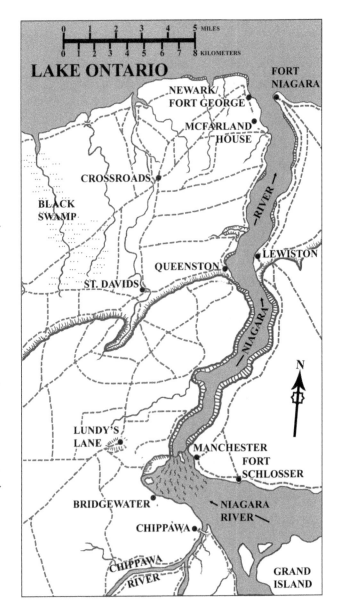

The lower (northern) half of the Niagara River.

(Fifth Regiment), volunteers from the Second Artillery Regiment, volunteers from the local Buffalo militias (under Dr. Cyrenius Chapin), and seamen (led by Lieutenant Jesse Elliot, USN).[*8]

Around eight o'clock in the evening of the 8th, the boats, manned by the naval volunteers, left the Scajaquada Creek* and rowed upriver under the cover of the American shoreline and into the Buffalo Creek, where the volunteer troops embarked. However, upon setting off, the now heavily laden boats were unable to pass over the sandbar at the entrance of the creek. The only recourse was for the majority of the men to strip off their equipment and climb over the side, wade alongside the boats, and push them into the deeper water so they could re-board. Soaking wet and shivering with the cold, the only way the men were able to keep warm was by rowing for the next few hours as the boats slowly edged out into Lake Erie and passed entirely around the enemy vessels in order to come at them from the Fort Erie side of the lake. Approaching the *Detroit* and *Caledonia* in silence, the Americans were challenged and then fired on by the British crews. Rapidly coming alongside, the American troops swarmed aboard and, after a

---

*Also referred to in original documents by the name: Scoijoiquoides, Scajaquadies, Scadjaquada, Conjocketty, Conjecitors, Conguichity, Conjocta, and Unnekuga Creek.

CAPTURE OF THE *DETROIT* AND *CALEDONIA*[*8]

American Force

Boat 1:
Second Artillery Regiment (Lieutenant Isaac Roach)
U.S Navy (Lieutenant Jesse Elliot)
Fifth Regiment (Ensign Prestman)
Total: 50 All Ranks

Boat 2:
Second Artillery Regiment (Captain Nathan Towson)
U.S Navy (Sailing Master George Watts)
Buffalo Militia (Captain Cyrenius Chapin)
Total: 50 All Ranks

American Casualties

Killed: 4 Other Ranks
Wounded: 2 Officers, 6 Other Ranks

British Casualties

Killed and Wounded: Unknown
Prisoner: 3 Officers, 55 crewmen

(N.B. According to one American account, twenty-seven American prisoners aboard the boats were also freed in the raid.)

brief but intense hand-to-hand fight, overwhelmed the two ship's crews. According to the later recollections of Lieutenant Roach (Second Artillery), a member of the boarding party attacking the *Detroit*:

In five minutes we were in possession and our prisoners driven below, and the hatchways secured. Some hands were sent aloft to loose the Topsails whilst I examined the Brig's guns and found them loaded ... I ordered them all hauled over to the starboard side ... to be ready for an attack from the shore.[9]

Onshore, the crews of the shore batteries heard the firing and, once the noise subsided, hailed the vessels, demanding to know what had happened. Upon receiving no response, they assumed the worst and opened fire.

Whiz comes a shot over our heads. John Bull always aims too high. This went about 20 feet over us, ricocheh'd and as our shore was lined with friends anxiously waiting ... killed Major Cuyler of the Militia whilst sitting on horseback ... Bang! Went my battery of 6 pounders, Up Helm Boys! Stand by that cable with the axe.[10]

After cutting the anchor cables, the prize crews steered the two vessels toward safety at Buffalo. Unluckily, as they manoeuvred the prevailing wind died and the two ships were caught and dragged downstream by the Niagara River's strong current, thus coming under additional heavy fire from the British artillery batteries lining the shore. In attempting to break away from this damaging barrage, the *Detroit* ran aground on Squaw Island, giving the British the opportunity to send a boatload of troops to recapture the vessel, but without success. After much cannonading by both sides and repeated attempts to possess the vessel made by parties from both armies, the Americans finally set it on fire, leaving it a gutted wreck. Similarly, while the *Caledonia* was towed under the cover of Winfield Scott's artillery battery at Black Rock, preventing its recapture, it came under a heavy cannonade from the British guns and suffered significant damage while tied up at the dock, making it unseaworthy for the foreseeable future.

Hearing of this success, Van Rensselaer's subordinates called on him to match the events at Buffalo; threatening that unless their men received orders to go into action they would desert and that he could find himself under suspicion of deliberately sabotaging the American war effort.[11] Consequently, Van Rensselaer ordered the invasion for the night of October 11–12.*[12] Leaving their respective encampments around Fort Niagara under conditions of freezing rain, gale force winds, and hail, the troops marched in strict silence along the single mud-choked trackway that led to

AMERICAN FORCES, NIAGARA FRONTIER, OCTOBER 12, 1812[12]

Lewiston

Regular: Lieutenant Colonel Fenwick, 550 All Ranks
　　　　Lieutenant Colonel Chrystie, 350 All Ranks
Militia: Brigadier General Miller, 558 All Ranks
　　　　Brigadier General Wadsworth, 1,682 All Ranks

Black Rock and Buffalo

Regular: Brigadier General Smyth, 1,650 All Ranks
Militia: Lieutenant Colonel Swift and Lieutenant
　　　　Colonel Hopkins, 386 All Ranks

Lewiston. Upon arriving at the embarkation point, however, they learned that the officer in charge of the boats had disappeared, supposedly taking with him a boat and all the available oars for the flotilla. Left with no means of propelling themselves across the river, the men were forced to endure a further gruelling march back to their encampments before attempting to dry off and await further orders. Despite this debacle and fearing that further delays would result in the complete disintegration of his military force, Van Rensselaer determined to mount his attack the following night — once some oars had been found.

Meanwhile, on the British side of the river, Major General Brock was well pleased with his level of preparedness in case of invasion. Following his victory at Detroit, much of the pro-American element of the Upper Canada population had been temporarily silenced, and numbers of the more vocal critics of Brock's administration had deemed it prudent to leave the province altogether. At the same time, the local militias and Native allies were heartened by the victory and expressed an increased willingness to join the affray. Brock also ensured that his limited number of regular troops were disposed to those points deemed under threat and additional defensive positions were prepared at strategic points along the riverbank.[13]

Since the beginning of the month, reconnaissance reports had noted substantial increases in the size of the American troop encampments on the opposite shore. There was also evidence of preparations within Fort Niagara, where the sloped roof of the old three-storey "Mess House" had been removed and the top floor converted into a raised artillery platform. Elsewhere, several new gun batteries were being constructed between Fort Niagara and a position that stood on top of the escarpment overlooking Lewiston (Fort Gray). Initially expecting that any American landing would take place at the mouth of the river and under the cover of the guns at Fort Niagara, the attack at Queenston was uncovered by Major Thomas Evans (8th [King's] Regiment), whilst delivering a message from Brock under a flag of truce.

BRITISH/CANADIAN FORCES, NIAGARA FRONTIER, OCTOBER 1812[*13]

(N.B. Numbers of troops can only be estimated due to variability in original listings.)

Fort George (Major Evans)

41st Regiment (Captain William Derenzy), 280 All Ranks
Royal Artillery (Captain William Holcroft), 35 All Ranks
Royal Engineers (Captain Henry Vigouroux), 6 All Ranks
1st/4th Lincoln Militia (Captain William Crooks), 200 All Ranks
1st/3rd York Militia (Captain Duncan Cameron), 120 All Ranks
Volunteer Coloured Corps (Captain Robert Runchey), 40 All Ranks
Niagara Light Dragoons (Major Thomas Merritt), 25 All Ranks
Volunteer Native Warriors (John Norton), 300 Warriors
Car Brigade (W. Crowther), 10 All Ranks

Brown's Point

3rd York Militia (Captain Duncan Cameron), 20 All Ranks

Vrooman's Point

2nd York Militia (Lieutenant Archibald McLean), 15 All Ranks

Queenston (Captain Dennis)

Royal Artillery (Sergeant Edlerton), 10 All Ranks
41st Regiment (Lieutenant William Crowther), 10 All Ranks
49th Regiment, Grenadier Company (Captain James Dennis), 95 All Ranks
 Light Company (Captain John Williams), 95 All Ranks
5th Lincoln Militia (Captain Stephen Hatt), 50 All Ranks
 (Captain James Durand), 50 All Ranks
2nd York Militia (Captain John Chisholm), 40 All Ranks
 (Captain William Applegarth), 40 All Ranks
1st Lincoln Militia Artillery (Lieutenant John Ball), 40 All Ranks

Chippawa (Captain Richard Bullock)

41st Regiment (Captain Bullock), 330 All Ranks
Royal Artillery (from Captain Holcroft's Coy), 15 All Ranks
2nd Lincoln Militia, (Lieutenant Colonel Thomas Clark), 100 All Ranks

Library and Archives Canada, C-99561.

(Above) *Fort Niagara*, J.E. Woolford, artist, circa 1821. Fort Niagara, as seen from alongside a Canadian battery position located at Newark. (Below) The same view in 2012.

Initially considering Evans as an alarmist, General Brock later decided to take no chances and ordered the various positions around Queenston to be fully alert for an imminent attack. He also sought to increase his militia forces, although he had little confidence in their military value due to American sympathizers within their ranks:

> The vast number of troops which have been added this day to the strong force

previously collected on the opposite side convinces me, with other indications, that an attack is not far distant. I have in consequence directed every exertion to be made to complete the militia to two thousand men, but I fear I shall not be able to effect my object with willing, well-disposed characters. Were it not for the number of Americans in our ranks we might defy all their efforts against this part of the Province.[14]

— Major General Brock to Sir George Prevost, October 12, 1812

From the American perspective, preparations for the crossing were not proceeding smoothly. First, although the invasion force of regulars had been supplemented with several regiments of New York State militia,[*15] the reality was that the Sixteenth N.Y. (Lieutenant Colonel Farrand

Stranahan) and Seventeenth N.Y. (Lieutenant Colonel Thompson Mead) were almost entirely without ammunition, or even cartridge boxes to carry any ammunition. Furthermore, detachments of men from the Eighteenth N.Y. (Major John Morrison) and Twentieth N.Y. (Lieutenant Colonel

---

AMERICAN UNITS, BATTLE OF QUEENSTON HEIGHTS, OCTOBER 13, 1812[*15]

Regular Army

Thirteenth Regiment (Lieutenant Colonel Chrystie)
Sixth Regiment (Captain McChesney)
Twenty-third Regiment (Major Mullany)
Artillery (Lieutenant Colonel J. Fenwick)
First Artillery Regiment (Lieutenant Gansevoort)
Second Artillery Regiment (Lieutenant Colonel Winfield Scott)
Third Artillery Regiment (Lieutenant Bayly)
Light Artillery Regiment (Captain Gibson)

New York State Militia

Sixteenth Regiment (Lieutenant Colonel Stranahan)
Seventeenth Regiment (Lieutenant Colonel Mead)
Eighteenth Regiment (Major Morrison)
Nineteenth Regiment (Lieutenant Colonel Bloom)
Twentieth Regiment (Lieutenant Colonel Allen)

Independent Companies and Detached Sections

Hopkin's Regiment
Moseley's Battalion of Militia Rifle Companies

Facing page (above): *Fort Niagara*, H. Slade, artist. This postwar view of Fort Niagara shows the garrison as it appeared during the war, with the roofs of the "French Castle" and blockhouses removed to facilitate the mounting of artillery. The main (riverside) gate of the fort from 1812–15 can be clearly seen, as can the (by then collapsing) perimeter picket walls. (Below) The same view in 2012.

Peter Allen) regiments were standing on their constitutional rights not to be used outside of the boundaries of the state, and refusing to cross into Canada. Second, while over sixty boats were within transportation range, only thirteen, each able to carry around twenty-five men, had been assembled to carry the troops across the river. In consequence, a shuttle service would be required to ferry the troops in waves, thus weakening the assault capability of the attackers. Third, what were conspicuous by their absence were the regular troops of Brigadier General Smyth. These units had begun their movement toward Lewiston, but had been turned back when the initial landing was cancelled. Now they were ordered by Smyth to remain at Buffalo. Finally, although a plan of embarkation had been devised, and was under the supervision of Lieutenant Colonel Solomon Van Rensselaer (a cousin to Stephen Van Rensselaer), the need for silence, coupled with the confusion of multiple units arriving in the darkness, led to a situation where the men of several companies from the Thirteenth Regiment simply loaded en masse, pushing aside many of the militia actually scheduled for the initial embarkation. Despite these fundamental flaws in operational planning, the loading of the boats took place and in the blackness of the night, the initial wave pushed out for the opposite shore — the invasion had begun.

From *Pictorial Field Book of the War of 1812.*

Colonel Solomon Van Rensselaer (artist unknown). Cousin to General Simon Van Rensselaer and military commander of the initial American attack at Queenston.

CHAPTER 6

Plans Gone Wrong, The Battle of Queenston Heights, October 13, 1812

Emerging from the shelter of the bank, the thirteen heavily laden boats were hard pressed to maintain formation within the strong river current.Attempting to avoid the known positions of the enemy in the village itself, the convoy aimed for a landing upstream, directly below the escarpment and in a dead zone below the firing arc covered by the "redan" battery on the hillside overlooking the village. Unfortunately, the strong mid-river current carried several boats downstream until they reached calmer waters near the Canadian shore, where they were able to begin the strenuous task of rowing back upstream toward the rest of the flotilla. According to a later account, the leading boat, containing Colonel Van Rensselaer and men from Captain Armstrong and Captain Malcolm's companies

View at Queens Town of West Landing, Upper Canada, Sempronius Stretton, artist, 1805. The Hamilton House is prominent in this early view of Queenston, as are the "heights" and Portage Road, winding its way up the escarpment. The redan battery would later be built just below the right-hand sweeping curve of the road.

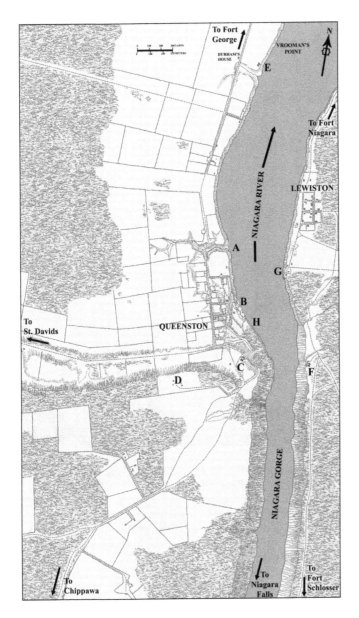

THE BATTLE OF QUEENSTON HEIGHTS, OCTOBER 13, 1812

A Hamilton Dock and Landing
B Queenston Government Dock
C Redan Battery
D Government Hospital and Barracks
E Vrooman's Point Battery
F Fort Gray Battery
G Lewiston Dock (U.S. 1812 invasion embarkation point)
H U.S. 1812 invasion initial landing point

Facing page: (Above) *Huts near the landing (Queenston)*, E. Simcoe, artist, circa 1793. The government dock at the village of Queenston in 1793, as seen from immediately above the 1812 American embarkation point. The American landing zone at the foot of the escarpment is to the left, hidden behind the rising ground and two tree stumps. (Below) The "landing" in 2012.

Plans Gone Wrong, The Battle of Queenston Heights, October 13, 1812

… reached the British shore before any of the others … and … remained under the bank unobserved for the space of five minutes; which time the officers employed in creeping up the bank for the purpose of reconnoitring the ground…. The men in the boat, being left to themselves, and dispensing with the restraint which their superiors had thus far required in imposing silence, began talking audibly, & the presence of the party was soon detected by a British sentinel posted upon the very bank from which the reconnaissance had been sought, tho' somewhat to the right of the boat at which he fired, wounding a Sergeant of Cap't Malcolm's Company — the sentinel to the left next fired, & thus, in quick succession the alarm was extended along the whole river front — The bugler upon the Heights then sounded it, & immediately after, that battery opened.[1]

To the men still rowing across the river, the dark outline of the approaching riverbank must have seemed to explode as the defending units and supporting artillery opened fire. Behind them, the American support batteries at Lewiston and Fort Gray also opened up once the element of surprise

was lost. Through this hail of crossfire, the boats pulled onto shore and those troops not already wounded piled out into the cold water of the river before scrambling up onto the slippery riverside embankment and the main landing dock occupied by British troops.

> The assailants quickly ascended the bank, & on reaching the plateau endeavoured to form line, but the darkness was extreme, and this, rendering both noise and confusion … attendant upon their efforts to effect an organisation, their precise position was not long a secret to two British Companies … who from flank positions … opened a crossfire upon their front — Under this state of things, it was evident the American party had no time for delay — their men were falling fast and a line was hastily, if not very scrupulously formed.[2]

There was nowhere to go but forward, and despite having been wounded in the ankle while still in the boat, Van Rensselaer led his troops to clear the riverbank of the enemy before the second wave arrived. After a brief but intense firefight, the defenders were initially forced to retreat into the village, but soon returned with reinforcements and a small artillery piece, forcing the American line, itself partially reinforced and now under the supervising command of Captain John Wool (Thirteenth Infantry), to reposition to face this new threat.

> Capt' Wool, without waiting for orders from Col. VanRanslaer, immediately changed his front, pivoting upon his right. With his small arms against the enemy's artillery and musketry, commenced his military career by throwing a well directed fire into the [enemy]…. A short but sharp contest now commenced in which the line-firings quickly succeeding each other were followed by cheers & were interchanged by both parties respectively.[3]

After another round of fierce gunfire, both sides retired to regroup. Having now been wounded a further five times and having suffered the loss of five of his senior officers, along with some twenty-five to thirty men, Colonel Van Rensselaer was compelled to order a retreat toward the American landing area, where he looked for Lieutenant Colonel Chrystie (Thirteenth Infantry) to hand over command. However the lieutenant colonel was nowhere to be found. In fact, the unfortunate officer was back on the U.S. side of the river.

During the crossing, Chrystie's boat had been one of those that had been swept downstream and come under musket fire. In a panic, the boat's pilot swung the boat away, back into midstream. Fighting with the pilot for control of the boat, Chrystie attempted to rejoin the flotilla, but soon recognized the futility of rowing up against the strong current. Beaching the boat on the American shore, well downriver of Lewiston, Chrystie walked back up the riverbank to join the next wave. Upon his arrival at the dockside, he was horrified to see

> … a scene of confusion hardly to be described. The enemy concentrated their fire upon our embarking place; no person being charged with directing the boats and embarkation or with the government of the boatmen, they forsook their duty. Persons unacquainted with the river … would occasionally hurry into a boat as they could find one, cross and leave it on the shore, perhaps to go adrift or else to be brought back by the wounded and their attendants and others returning without order or permission; and these would land where they found it convenient and leave the boat where they landed.[4]

— Lieutenant Colonel Chrystie to General Cushing, February 22, 1813

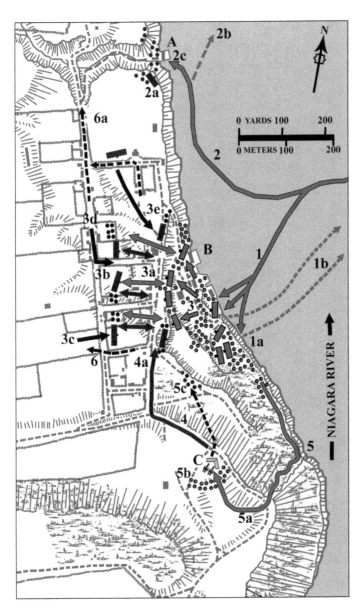

The American landings, stalemate in the village, and the capture of the redan battery.

A   Hamilton Dock and Landing
B   Queenston Government Dock
C   Redan Battery

6:00 a.m. – 7:30 a.m.

1. Under cover of darkness, U.S. boats cross the Niagara River from Lewiston (1), but are detected. Under increasing fire from the British defenders, the first wave lands at the foot of the escarpment (1a) and push up the slope of the riverbank, engaging the defenders, while the boats return for the second wave (1b).

2. During successive crossings, several boats are swept downstream (2) and come under fire from troops (2a) at Hamilton's dock (B) causing multiple casualties. Some boats veer away (2b) while others are forced to land (2c) and become prisoners.

3. U.S. units continue to push up from the landing ground (3) and engage British units attempting to bottle-up the American beachhead in a fierce firefight in the village (3a). This initially forces the British to retire (3b) but the Americans are unable to break out from the landing ground and become trapped once additional British reinforcements arrive (3c, 3d, 3e).

4. General Brock arrives from Fort George to find the British/Canadian troops containing the Americans but under strong pressure. In response, he orders the detachment of the 49th Regiment (Light Company) (4) down from the Redan battery (C), to engage the Americans (4a).

5. U.S troops under Captain John Wool locate and climb the Fisherman's path (5, 5a), storm the redan battery from the rear (5b), forcing the artillerists to spike their guns and escape downhill (5c).

6. With increased daylight, the British forces come under heavy artillery fire from U.S. artillery batteries at Fort Gray and Lewiston and are eventually forced to abandon their positions and retreat to the north end of the village (6, 6a).

Queenston, O. Staples, artist (after E. Simcoe), 1913. Looking south to Queenston from the strategic vantage point of the Vrooman's Point battery location in 1792.

Despite these difficulties, boats filled with men made the dangerous crossing, only to either join Van Rensselaer's troops trapped along the shore, or be pulled downstream by the current and come under heavy fire from additional defenders stationed on the dock below the Hamilton house near the northern end of the village. Two of these boats, both containing a high proportion of officers, suffered enough casualties that they floated helplessly ashore and fell immediately into the hands of the waiting Canadian militia. Others attempted to make a landing at the dock but were soon overwhelmed by the defenders, after a stiff firefight that left many of the American's dead or wounded. The situation had all the makings of a disaster of the first magnitude. Back on the embattled beach, Solomon Van Rensselaer initially considered a frontal attack on the massing troops before him. Instead, he and Captain Wool determined that the only hope was to attempt a flanking movement toward the angle

of the escarpment where it entered the gorge of the Niagara River — where they had information that there was a rough path, commonly used by fishermen at what was locally referred to as the "point-of-the-rock" (where the east-west line of the escarpment meets the north-south line of the Niagara Gorge) that would allow them to gain the high ground behind the hillside redan artillery battery. With nothing to lose, the troops slipped off into the darkness in search of the path.

On the other side of the village, things appeared reasonably under control to Major General Brock. Awoken at Fort George by the distant thunder of gunfire, the commander had ridden post-haste from

The same vantage in 2012. Including the relative movement of the American forces and various positions at the time of the battle.

B   Queenston Government Dock
C   Redan Battery
D   Government Hospital and Barracks
E   Vrooman's Point Battery
F   Fort Gray Battery
G   Lewiston Dock (U.S. 1812 invasion embarkation point)
H   U.S. 1812 invasion, initial landing point

1. U.S. forces (1) embark at Lewiston (G) and make their initial landing (1a) (H) above the Government Dock (B).
2. Pushing back the initial opposition (2), the Americans move up into the village and engage the defenders (2a). Following a series of engagements, the Americans are forced back to the riverbank (2b).
3. Looking to outflank the defenders, U.S. detachments (3) move up the riverbank and locate the "Fisherman's Path" (3a). They climb the hill (3b) and assault the redan battery (C) from the rear (3c).

the fort, without waiting for either his troops or his aides. As he rode toward Queenston, he ordered each detachment of troops that he passed to march to the sound of the guns. Arriving at Queenston, he saw with pride that his greatly outnumbered regulars were holding the Americans in check, while the local militias were proving their loyalty by turning out in numbers greater than he had predicted. Despite this, matters still hung in the balance and, certain that further waves of Americans would cross over, Brock looked for reinforcements. By his own orders, his main troop concentrations had been retained at

Fort George in case the attack on Queenston was a diversion; but this was obviously no feint and even if he ordered them up immediately, they could not be expected for some time. Meanwhile, to his front, the British and Canadian troops penning in the Americans were coming under increasing pressure from the enemy's growing strength as additional reinforcements arrived. In response, Brock went up to the hillside battery and ordered his only disposable force, the Light Company of the 49th (Captain John Williams), to join the troops below instead of covering the hilltop and rear of the redan battery on the escarpment. With this small augmented force, Brock's men inflicted severe casualties amongst the Americans on the waterfront. However, the redeployment exposed the redan battery and the entire British south flank to an attack, *if* the Americans could reach the heights, which of course no one, least of all Brock, considered possible while the Americans were seemingly being successfully pinned down on the riverbank.

Unfortunately, this was exactly what Wool *had* succeeded in doing. Gathering almost 200 men from the Sixth, Thirteenth, and Twenty-third Regiments, plus a gun crew from the New York Militia Artillery, Captain Wool's force had scaled the heights and emerged on the higher ground just above and behind the redan battery. From there, the Americans swooped down on the unsuspecting artillerymen.

View from Queenston Heights, G. Heriot, artist, circa 1805. The view from the Portage Road, drawn just downhill from the redan battery. The government dock is visible at bottom right and the road through Queenston [Front Street] at left.

Library and Archives Canada, C-012772.

After a short resistance that caused casualties on both sides, the surviving British gunners "spiked" their 18-pounder gun, rendering it inoperable, before scrambling down the slope toward the village below, along with their discomfited commander.

With the increasing light of day, the position for the British and Canadian defenders became serious. Behind them, the Americans controlled the heights; before them, increasing numbers of Americans were massing along the riverbank as more boats crossed from Lewiston; but most dangerously, the increasing visibility of the morning allowed the American gun batteries at Lewiston and Fort Gray to locate and target any points of resistance by the defenders. In short order, a number of the British guns, which had so devastated the American boats, were either disabled or forced to withdraw. In a similar fashion, the already depleted ranks of the infantry came under increased fire and seemed likely to break unless matters improved. Recognizing that a crisis had arisen, and determined to regain the dominant heights in order to create a stronghold for further resistance until reinforcements arrived, General Brock did not waste time issuing orders. Instead, he personally rode around the village, gathering together a composite force from his regular and militia detachments. With his force assembled, Brock led his troops into the open ground beyond the Secord farm at the base of the hillside. Advancing toward the American left flank, Brock's force came under a brisk musket fire from the front line of American skirmishers covering the hillside and the captured gun position. After an intense firefight, the Americans were able to halt the British advance. Seeking to maintain the initiative, Brock dismounted from his horse, rallied his men, and moved out in front of his troops, perhaps forgetting that the primary responsibility of a senior commander is to remain in a position to direct a victory and not get involved in trying to create it. As a result, isolated in front of the line and wearing

the highly distinctive uniform of a British senior officer, he suffered the consequences when an American soldier took aim and shot General Brock through the chest.

Stunned and outraged at the sight of their commander falling mortally wounded, Brock's troops pressed forward, but made no headway against the secure positions of the Americans. Eventually, under a heavy fire, they collected the general's body and withdrew down the slope. Shortly afterwards, the general's aide, Lieutenant Colonel John Macdonell,

Unable to acquire the actual ground, the 1850s committee looking to erect a monument to mark the point where General Brock actually fell were forced to locate it almost two blocks away. Therefore, they inscribed the location as being located *"Near this spot."* Not, as popular history has it, halfway up the hill towards the redan battery, but down slope, nearer to the Secord family home and present-day museum.

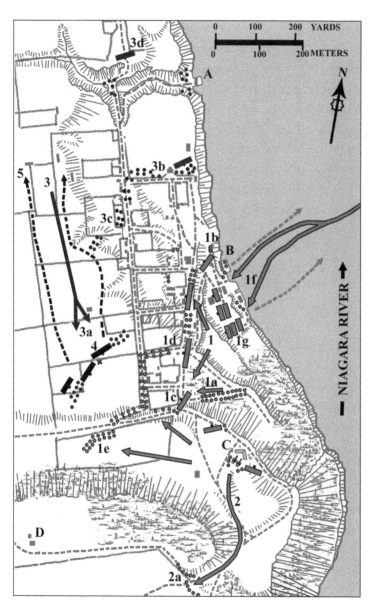

General Brock's counterattack to regain the captured guns

7:30 a.m. – 8:30 a.m.

1. U.S. units move out of the beachhead into the village (1, 1a) and establish a perimeter of skirmishers among the houses and gardens (1b, 1c) while those at the redan battery (C) form a skirmish line running from the village up onto the hillside (1d, 1e). Successive waves of reinforcements land and take up positions to secure the village (1f, 1g).

2. U.S. detachments move up the escarpment (2) and secure the Queenston-Chippawa Portage Road (2a).

3. General Brock gathers a composite force of detachments at the north end of Queenston (3). He then marches his line across the open ground behind the village (3a), while additional units maintain pressure on the American perimeter (3b, 3c) and secure the main road (3d).

4. After the British/Canadian advance is halted by American fire (4), General Brock moves out in front of his line and is shot while rallying his men (X).

5. The British/Canadian force retreats back to the north end of the village (5).

attempted to revenge the death of his commander and succeed where his leader had failed, by organizing a second assault on the hill that took a more circuitous route in an attempt to flank the battery position. Initially, this assault succeeded in pressing the Americans back up the slope to the earthworks of the redan battery, causing the Americans inside to spike one of the guns that they had only just cleared. But just as his commander had suffered for his bravery, so too did Macdonell. He fell, shot through the belly. Within moments, the offensive collapsed and a counterattack by the Americans threw the weakened and disheartened British/Canadian troops back down the hill. Effective resistance to the invasion all but collapsed and individual units withdrew from the village as best they could, attempting to regroup downriver at Vrooman's Point. On the other side of the village, the Americans began to solidify their position and establish a secure bridgehead for further troops to land. However, back on the American side of the river, less than a half-dozen boats remained to ferry the waiting regiments to the Canadian shore. Consequently, the reinforcement of the American beachhead had slowed to a crawl. Nevertheless, it appeared that despite all their earlier blunders, the Americans had carried the day and the battle was won. Finally, a victory could be reported to Washington.

As the morning progressed, additional detachments augmented Captain Wool's command on the heights. He even gained some artillery support in the form of a 6-pounder cannon and ammunition limber. This piece had been laboriously dismantled, transported across the river, re-assembled, and then hauled up the escarpment by men from Captain James Gibson's Light Artillery Company. As such, it was a welcome addition to the extended lines that the Americans sought to establish on top of the escarpment and astride the road leading from Queenston to Chippawa. However, Captain Wool had suffered a wound at the onset of the fighting and, due to blood loss, was forced to relinquish his command, which was taken up by Lieutenant Colonel Chrystie. Shortly thereafter, Brigadier General Wadsworth joined the force on the hilltop, becoming the senior officer. The general also brought news that there were still a significant number of militiamen that were refusing to cross the Niagara. As a result, Lieutenant Colonel Chrystie was ordered to cross back to the U.S. side of the river, locate Major General Stephen Van Rensselaer, and impress upon him the urgent necessity of getting these recalcitrant troops onto the battlefield.

Meanwhile, at the north end of the village, grievous as the death of Brock was to the morale of the surviving British and Canadian troops, it actually engendered a thirst for revenge on the part of the soldiers, not a desire to flee. In consequence, the remnants of the defenders remained at Vrooman's

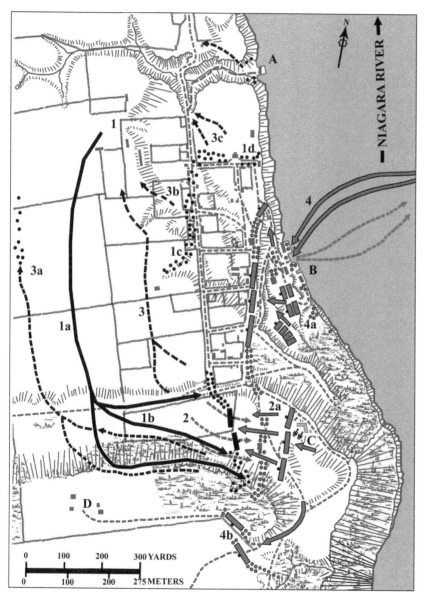

Lieutenant Colonel John Macdonell's counterattack.

8:30 a.m. – 9:30 a.m.

1. Lieutenant Colonel Macdonell rallies the defending troops (1) and makes a wide sweep to the west (1a) before attacking the Americans along the slope of the escarpment above the village (1b), while militia detachments secure his flank (1c, 1d).

2. The American skirmish line (2) is pressed back up the hill toward the redan battery (C), forcing them to spike the guns again. Once Lieutenant Colonel Macdonell is shot, the attack falters, allowing the Americans to mount a counterattack (2a) that drives the British/Canadian troops off the hill.

3. All British/Canadian units (3, 3a, 3b, 3c) withdraw north from Queenston toward Vrooman's Point.

4. With a greatly reduced number of boats (4), the Americans continue to build up their forces in the village (4a) while additional units move up onto the escarpment to secure the American positions from counterattack from Chippawa (4b).

Point awaiting orders. Shortly afterward, a band of nearly 200 Native warriors, led by their war chief John Norton (Teyoninhokovrawen), arrived at the battlefield, staying close to the heavy woods west of the village. Meeting with some of the retreating militia and hearing of Brock's death, many of Norton's warriors took this retreat as a signal for their own withdrawal and melted into the woods. Still determined to advance, Norton heartened his remaining band of about eighty warriors and led his men in a flanking movement to the right, eventually passing around the American perimeter and reaching the top of the escarpment. Moving across the Chippawa road toward the American left flank, Norton sent a messenger to the British garrison at Chippawa for assistance; he then dispersed his warriors under cover of the trees and began sniping at the Americans. Startled by the sudden war cries and firing from the woods on their flank and rear, Lieutenant Colonel Winfield Scott (Second U.S. Artillery), who had left his own assigned post on the American side of the river to join in on the attack,

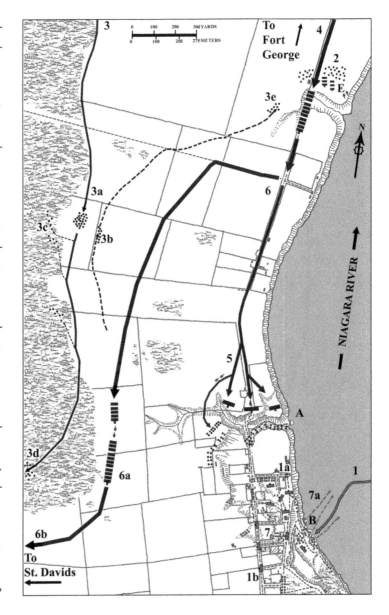

The detour routes taken first by the Native warriors, led by John Norton and later by General Sheaffe's column to gain the heights to attack the Americans from the rear (south).

9:30 a.m. – Noon.

1. U.S. reinforcements continue to land (1) at the government dock (B) and push out their defensive perimeter to the edge of the village (1a, 1b).

2. British/Canadian troops (2) at the Vrooman's Point battery (E) await reinforcements from Fort George.

3. Native forces under John Norton arrive (3) and move south following the treeline of the forest (3a). Hearing of Brock's death from some militia retreating toward Vrooman's Point (3b), many warriors abandon the advance (3c). A core group of approximately eighty warriors continue the advance west to reach a pathway (off map) that leads up the escarpment (3d). The militia detachment continues its retreat toward the assembly area at Vrooman's Point (3e).

4. General Sheaffe arrives with reinforcements at Vrooman's Point (4), and deciding against a direct frontal assault, directs a two-pronged counterattack be made by all the assembled force.

5. Canadian militia and Holcroft's artillery advance directly toward the village to fix the American units below the escarpment in place (5).

6. General Sheaffe's column moves across country in a wide detour (6, 6a, 6b) to connect with the Queenston-St. Davids Road (off map) and follow Norton's route to the top of the escarpment.

7. The American ferry system collapses as American units refuse to cross, while increasing numbers of American troops abandon their positions (7) and use whatever boats are available to escape back across the Niagara River (7a), only to come under fire from Vrooman's battery.

Lieutenant Colonel Winfield Scott. Placed in charge of artillery at Lewiston, he subsequently left his designated post (without orders) to join the invasion, and led the American forces in a succession of fruitless bayonet charges against the British Native harassing attacks.

thought he was being attacked by forces coming from Chippawa. Without orders, he took it upon himself to take command of the troops at that end of the line and establish a line of defence facing south from behind a fence (that separated the open farm fields from the partially wooded military reservation lands that followed the line of the escarpment). Under continued fire, Scott ordered his composite force of infantrymen to make a bayonet charge to clear the enemy Native warriors from his flank. However, while the initial advance forced the Natives to retire, they simply regrouped further to the American right and attacked again. This forced Scott to respond with a series of charges that eventually ended up with his force standing at the edge of the slope of the escarpment overlooking the village of Queenston. Unable to drive off the Natives or fortify their dominating position whilst under fire, Scott and his troops were forced to retire back to the wood line to put more open ground between themselves and the repeated probes of the warriors. By now, Major General Sheaffe had arrived at Vrooman's Point with the reinforcements from Fort George and was also preparing to advance on the American lines. In addition, a new artillery piece had arrived (Captain William Holcroft) and, joining with the other guns situated there, opened up on the remaining American boats — with deadly results.

The Native harassing attacks and Winfield Scott's counterattacks.

Noon – 1:00 p.m.

1. U.S. troops in Queenston (1) and on the lower slope of the escarpment (1a) attempt to maintain a weakening perimeter to control the village, as increasing numbers of men attempt to return to the American side of the river or hide along the riverbank (1b, 1c). Other units (1d) move up the escarpment from the redan battery (C) and join the main body of U.S. troops (1e, 1f) controlling the Portage Road and the high ground.

2. Reaching the top of the escarpment, Norton's warriors (2) move up under cover of the treeline, cross the Portage Road (2a) and commence a harassing attack (2b) on the American left flank (2c).

3. Lieutenant Colonel Winfield Scott, witnessing the British Native allies attacking the left flank, leads a body of formed troops in a bayonet charge (3) against the Natives, driving them off (3a). However, the Natives simply move to their left and regroup before attacking once again (3b). Winfield Scott is then forced to repeatedly move to this right and make a number of bayonet charges, while the Natives simply keep moving to their left and reengage at will (3c, 3d, 3e). Reaching the British hospital and barracks on the heights (D) both sides disengage, with part of the Native force remaining at the treeline (3f) above the escarpment, while others move down the slope (3g) to outflank the American positions above the village. Winfield Scott withdraws his forces to secure the American right flank (3h).

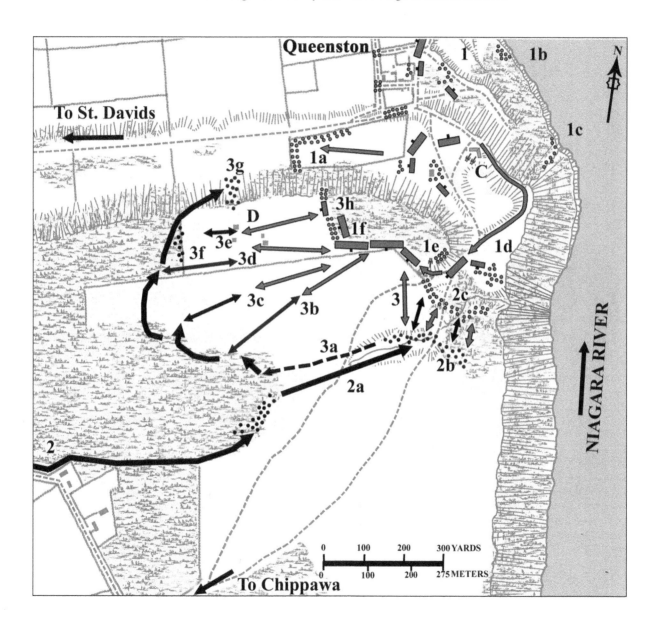

Queenston

To St. Davids

NIAGARA RIVER

To Chippawa

| 0 | 100 | 200 | 300 YARDS |
| 0 | 100 | 200 | 275 METERS |

N

Library and Archives Canada, C-111307.

Major General R.H. Sheaffe in later life. He was forty-nine years old in October 1812. Although the technical "victor" of the Battle of Queenston Heights, history has denied him the appropriate credit. Subsequently, as lieutenant governor of Upper Canada, Sheaffe was unable to maintain the alliances developed by Brock and came under increasing levels of criticism. He was eventually replaced and reassigned to Montreal in June 1813.

Hearing the renewed firing from the heights across the river, Major General Stephen Van Rensselaer finally undertook to join his troops on the Canadian shore. He was mortified, however, when those troops awaiting embarkment adamantly refused to board the boats with him. After studying the increasingly serious situation at the beachhead, he returned to the American side and rode post-haste to the main encampment to persuade the reserve of militia troops to march to their comrades' aid, only to be soundly rebuffed.

> … the mass of this … [militia] … was immovable. Neither entreaty nor threats — neither arguments nor ridicule availed anything. They had seen enough of war to satisfy them that it made no part of their special calling; and at last, not distaining to employ the mask, invented by factions to cover cowardice or treason, fifteen hundred able-bodied men, well armed and equipped, who a week before boasted loudly of patriotism and prowess, were now found openly pleading constitutional scruples in justification of disobedience to the lawful authority of their chief.[5]

Humiliated, Van Rensselaer was forced to return to the dock and pen a letter to his commanders on the Canadian side. In it he explained his inability to support their position with additional troops and suggested that if they were unable to retreat to the riverbank their surrender might become inevitable. By this time, the arriving British reinforcements had also been seen by the American perimeter troops in the village. In response, increasing numbers of men deserted their posts and began to filter back to the riverbank, where they endeavoured to recross the Niagara by any means possible. The American position around Queenston was weakening, but the heights were still firmly under the control of the bulk of the American force.

For his part, Major General Sheaffe studied the American positions and determined that repeating Brock's method of a direct frontal assault would bring needless casualties and probable failure. Instead, he decided to follow Norton's example, reach the heights by a circuitous route and attack downhill, while a smaller detachment and Holcroft's artillery held the Americans attention from the front. According to Captain James Crooks of the 1st Lincoln Militia:

On crossing the ravine at Durham's the fences were let down and we took a course to the right in the direction of St. Davids, where we found an old road ascending the mountain about two miles west of Queenston. Up this road we soon made the top and formed in a ploughed field.... We then moved on and took possession of the main road leading from Queenston to the Falls, there awaiting reinforcements that had been ordered from Chippawa.... Here we began to be pelted with shot from an 18 pounder battery on the opposite side of the river called Fort Gray, but it did no harm, the shot flying over us as we lay on the ground. It was rather trying for Militiamen who had never been in action to remain pelted with bullets from Fort Gray for more than an hour in the face of the enemy. The latter were posted in a young wood, where Brock's monument now stands, with a worm fence in front, and their bayonets glistening in the sun. At last, the order was given to advance and ... at the double quick we soon encountered the enemy.[6]

However, other accounts record that during the course of this hour-long pause Sheaffe unexpectedly issued new orders to several units, which manoeuvred their men by countermarching the column, as there was some perceived confusion of their unit alignment and proper frontage. Completing this complicated manoeuvre, in full view of the enemy, Sheaffe then deployed his force

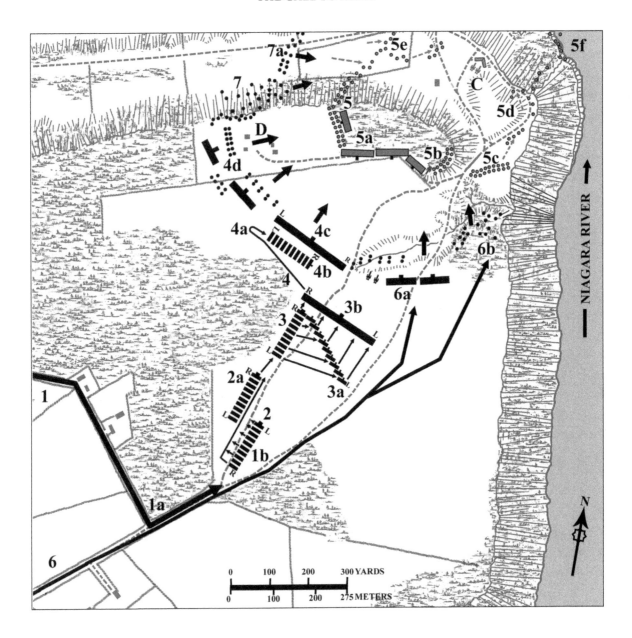

General Sheaffe's column arrives on the battlefield, redeploys, and countermarches in front of the enemy.

12:30 p.m – 2:30 p.m.
1. General Sheaffe's column reaches the top of the escarpment and advances (1) to the Portage Road and moves south (1a), heading toward the American positions. It then halts for almost an hour (1b), while under long-range artillery harassment from Fort Gray, to await the arrival of reinforcement units from Chippawa.

2. General Sheaffe decides that the main part of the column is in "clubbed" (reverse) sequence to his planned order of attack (i.e., with its left flank (L) in front) (2). He therefore orders its reordering to place the right flank (R) in front (2a).

3. Upon advancing, the broken ground and woods prevent a proper deployment of the column to the left into a (L-R) line (3). It is therefore forced to deploy in reverse order to the right (3a) causing the line to club (R-L) when it is formed (3b).

4. Forced to reorganize once more, Sheaffe reforms his column (R-L) (4) and marches it to the left (4a) and then countermarches to the right (L-R) (4b). The column then forms line to the front in the correct (L-R) sequence (4c). At the same time, the left wing of the British line extends to the escarpment (4d)

5. Surprisingly, the American line on the escarpment (5, 5a, 5b, 5c) makes no move to attack the British while they are reorganizing and vulnerable. Increasing numbers of Americans begin to abandon their positions and seek to return to the riverbank in order to find passage to the American side of the river (5d, 5e, 5f).

6. Reinforcements from Chippawa (6) arrive as the British line is finalizing its deployments. The Chippawa force extend the British line to the right (6a, 6b) as the entire British line advances and begins to fire on the Americans.

7. On the escarpment slope, the British Native allies (7) and Canadian militias (7a) also begin their main attack on the weakening American positions directly below the escarpment.

into line, only to realize that his initial formation was correct and that he had just inverted his proper fighting line with his left and right flanks reversed. Consequently, he was forced to order yet another countermarch to properly re-establish his battle formation, all the while having left his force totally vulnerable to an enemy counterattack. Fortunately for him, instead of taking advantage of this error of command, the bemused Americans simply stood and watched as the British force paraded up and down the field in front of them. According to American eyewitnesses of this extraordinary proceeding, they did not attack because they were convinced it was being done deliberately, either to intimidate them or to locate a potential weak spot that could be attacked. Finally taking up his desired position, Sheaffe placed the bulk of the 41st Regiment at the centre of his line with his small artillery pieces and several companies of militia in support. His left flank was secured by two companies of the 49th Regiment, while the steadfast band of

Indian warriors under Norton continued to undermine the resolve of the Americans with their incessant attacks, supported by a detachment of around a hundred men from the 41st Regiment, under Lieutenant McIntyre. On the other flank were more Natives and militia. In addition, word arrived that Captain Bullock was moving north with a force of regulars and militia from Chippawa. Little activity could be seen from the American lines on the other side of the small piece of open ground dividing the two forces and, not wanting to give the enemy more time to prepare than he already had, Sheaffe stood back and gave the order to advance. At this crucial moment, Bullock's troops arrived and immediately wheeled into position on the right flank, extending the British line into a wide arc of troops moving forward on a narrowing front and focussing on the American centre.

Outnumbered and isolated, the American line initially stood and opened fire on the advancing enemy. However, after trading several volleys, once Brigadier General Wadsworth decided to make a fighting withdrawal and ordered a retreat, all command structure collapsed, the American line folded, and it became was every man for himself. Some of the more dynamic commanders, like Winfield Scott and Chrystie, attempted to stem the rout. But eventually they too were forced to join their fellows in scrambling down the steep slopes of the escarpment,

The American invasion collapses as the British/Canadian/Native alliance press forward.

2:30 p.m. – 3:30 p.m.

1. The British/Canadian/Native line (1, 1a) advances upon the American line (1b, 1c) and the two formations engage in a close-range firefight for several volleys.

2. Under pressure from British Native allies and Canadian militia units (2, 2a), the American flanks start to waver and begin to retire (2b, 2c). U.S. General Wadsworth orders a fighting withdrawal to the boats. However, once the American retreat begins it rapidly degenerates into a rout (2d).

3. Below the escarpment, British regular and Canadian militia detachments press forward (3, 3a) as the American perimeter in the village collapses (3b).

4. The Americans are pressed into an ever-decreasing pocket (4) around the government dock (B), where groups of individuals attempt to escape in whatever boats remain afloat (4a), try to swim across the river (4b), or hide in the underbrush bordering the river to evade capture (4c). The battle ends with the surrender of the American beachhead.

to the sound of blood-curdling cries from the British Native allies and reverberations of musket fire from the militia and regulars harrying the Americans to their destruction. Numerous Americans were injured or killed in their precipitous descent to the village of Queenston and the riverbank, where some desperate individuals threw away their weapons and

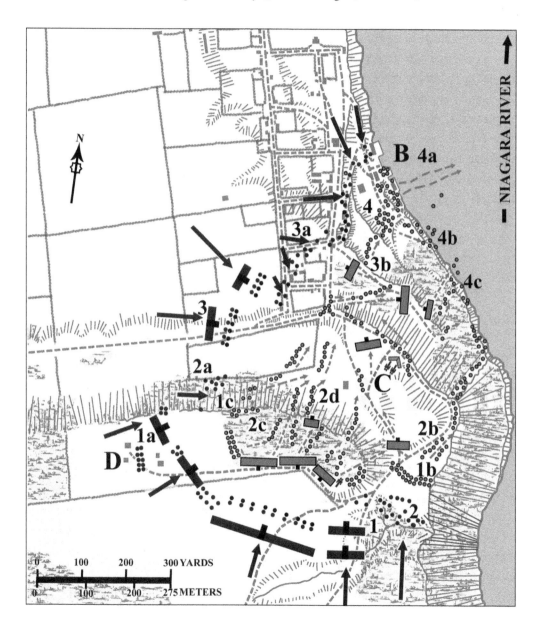

equipment and attempted to swim across the river. Few, if any, made it safely ashore on the American side, and accounts record the spectacle of flailing bodies being swept downstream in the grip of the cold river current toward Lake Ontario. For the majority, however, surrender was the only realistic option and at least two attempts were made to raise a white flag. Unfortunately, battle fever blinded some of the Allied troops and the unfortunate bearers of the flag were shot down. Eventually Winfield Scott brought matters to a close by seizing a white neck-cloth and holding it aloft on his sword as a sign of the American capitulation. In the aftermath of this final action, four participants recorded their impressions of these events:

> We was then ordered to advance; our little field pieces commenced firing. It was returned by the Americans with a six-pounder masked in the brush. A rapid advance was ordered, without firing a musket shot on our part, until within a small distance of the enemy under cover of the woods and underbrush. We was then ordered to halt and fire…. We stood but a short time until, I suppose, we was ordered to advance with double quick time. The musketry made such a noise I heard no order, but as the others moved we all followed…. The General and his aid, no doubt, as they ought to do, had a position that was clear to them, but as the wind blew from the enemy we had both their smoke and ours in our faces.[7]

— Private William Woodruff,
1st Lincoln Militia

> The Ground on which we had fought was well adapted to favour a small number against a stronger force. On our left, the steep descent of Queenstown mountain, along which & the meadows beneath, we had an uninterrupted view — on our right an extensive field, that reached to the Niagara River, which exposed to our Sight any Body of the Enemy that might advance in that Direction to pass our flank … General Sheaffe and the Troops — having now ascended the Hill … a Reinforcement of Light Infantry of one Hundred Men … of the 41st were sent to us … at the same time we were also strengthened by a number of Cuyugwa Warriors, who had been detained at Niagara…. We were thus more than doubly strengthened.

We arranged ourselves on the Extremity of the left — the Light Infantry taking post on our right — next to the Main Body. When we saw the right Wing enter the field — we rushed forward — the enemy fired — we closed & they ran; … we came upon them Swiftly — they left their cannon, & we raised the Shout of Victory. — they ran in disorder — many falling on the way … right along the Bank of the River — the Enemy disappeared under the Bank; many plunging into the River.[8]

— John Norton, Native warrior leader

On the advance I perceived an iron 6 pounder abandoned…. I ran to it with two or three men and turned it round upon a large group of Yankees in Lewiston, our own people being between it and the enemy on the heights [at Fort Gray] … and managed to discharge it several times towards the enemy at Lewiston…. The battle …was a very warm and close one. I have been in many hail storms, but never in one where the stones flew so thick as the bullets on this occasion…. The lines were very near each other, and every foot of the ground the enemy gave way gave us an advantage, as on their side it descended. After almost half an hour's close engagement they disappeared in the smoke, throwing down their arms, and ran down the heights to the water's edge in the vain hope of reaching their own side.[9]

— Captain James Crooks, 1st Lincoln Militia

I saw many of the American soldiers run and plunge down the bank, some went down upon the rocks and trees & were killed while many who plunged into the river were drowned, the river running at a very rapid rate. None but the most powerful swimmers succeeded in reaching the American shore.[10]

— Private John Chapman, 41st Regiment

The losses suffered by the American army in this battle are somewhat ambiguous. This situation is not surprising considering:

- the disorganized and broken nature of the units landing on the Canadian shore;

Brock's Monument as it looks today. The second one to be built, it marks the epicentre of the fighting at the climax of the Battle of Queenston Heights. The area, which was once a landscape of fields, farmsteads, military buildings, and dense forest, is now a manicured park that attracts tourists from around the globe.

- the confused mixture of regiments engaged in the various portions of the battle;
- the high level of desertions from the field and military encampments, both during and after the battle; and
- the unknown number of individuals who were swept away by the river when their boats sank beneath them in the initial assaults or during the chaos of the rout at the end of the battle.

Estimates are that only about one-third of the available troops actually crossed the river. Of these, over 900 ended up as prisoners. On the other side of the conflict, British official accounts record a far lower casualty roll.[*11] This disparity would normally stand as a glorious victory for the British, but the death of General Brock was credited as such a grievous loss that some contemporary accounts make more of this event than of the subsequent success of General Sheaffe in winning the battle.

In a sidebar to the battle, it must be noted that the garrisons at Fort George and Fort Erie were also engaged in combat during the course of the day. At Fort George, before dawn, as General Brock galloped toward Queenston, the American artillery at Fort Niagara opened up on the fort and the town alongside. Within a short time the town's jail, courthouse, and several homes and other civilian buildings were set ablaze, torched by the Americans using cannonballs cooked in a furnace until red-hot and then fired as "hot-shot." In return, the British artillery batteries at Fort George, supported by detached batteries sited along the riverbank, bombarded Fort Niagara, causing significant damage and forcing the artillerists to abandon their elevated positions on the fort buildings. In retaliation, the American detached batteries along the riverbank joined in and several hot-shot set fire to the wooden barracks and storehouses within the fort. Most dangerously, however, was the impact of a hot-shot on the roof of the fort's

ESTIMATE OF CASUALTIES, BATTLE OF QUEENSTON HEIGHTS, OCTOBER 13, 1812[*11]

British Regulars

Killed: 1 General Officer, 1 Sergeant, 9 Rank and File
Wounded: 2 Officers, 4 Sergeants, 38 Rank and File
Prisoner: 6 Rank and File

Canadian Militias

Killed: 1 Staff Officer, 2 Rank and File
Wounded: 2 Sergeants, 28 Rank and File
Prisoner: 5 Rank and File

Native Allies

At least 6 killed, 85 wounded, and 21 missing/ prisoner

American

Regular Officers: estimated 4 killed, 3 wounded, 4 wounded prisoners, 15 prisoners
State Militia Officers: estimated 2 killed, 5 wounded, 49 prisoners
Cumulative total, Killed, Wounded, Missing: Regulars and Militias: All Ranks estimated 100–500 (exact figures are unknown, while differing accounts come up with variable totals due to the broken nature of units involved, desertions, and losses in the Niagara River)
Cumulative total, known Prisoners: estimated Regulars: 19 Officers, 417 Other Ranks
estimated Militia: 54 Officers, 435 other Ranks

Above and right: Two views of the reconstructed National Historic site of Fort George as seen in 2012 from the American side of the Niagara River.

Facing page: (Above) *A View of Fort George Upper Canada*, E. Walsh, artist, circa 1813. Fort George as seen from a riverside American fortification upriver of Fort Niagara. The Navy Hall complex of buildings can be seen at centre left. (Below) Modern waterfront developments encroach on the same view of Fort George in 2012.

powder magazine. Piercing the roof's metal covering, the red-hot ball lodged within the wooden beams of the roof and began to burn its way through toward the large quantities of black powder below, threatening a devastating explosion. In response, many of the small number of troops left behind to guard the garrison made a quick exit through the fort's gate and headed for the cover of the nearby woods. Ignoring the danger, however, Captain Henry M. Vigoureux (Royal Engineers) and a handful of men clambered up onto the smouldering building and proceeded to tear away at the roofing to expose the shot. Creating a bucket chain, Vigoureux and his valiant crew doused the rising fires and extracted the still-warm cannonball, thus saving the fort from destruction. While at Fort Erie, once news reached the fort of the American attack at Queenston, the riverside batteries were ordered to begin a bombardment of the enemy positions in an effort to prevent them detaching troops to support the invasion. As part of this cannonade, an American barrack, containing a quantity of ammunition, exploded, killing and injuring several soldiers inside the building; a warehouse full of goods removed from the *Caledonia* was set on fire, severely damaging the salvaged goods; while the *Caledonia*, already damaged, was hit several more times and sank at her mooring.

Three days after the battle, on October 16, 1812, a solemn military funeral procession wound its

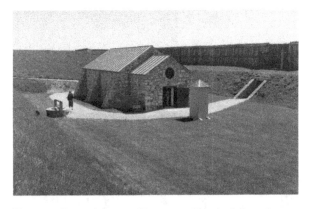

The powder and ammunition magazine building at Fort George. Hit by hot-shot on October 13, 1812, but saved from exploding by the heroism of Captain Henry Vigoureux (R.E) and his team of volunteers.

way from Government House to Fort George, where Major General Isaac Brock, and his aide Lieutenant Colonel John Macdonell, were interred with full military honours within the bank of one of the fort's bastions. The British artillery fired a salute to their fallen leader, which was shortly echoed by a similar volley from the American batteries across the river, along with their flag being flown at half-mast, a solemn sign of the esteem in which Brock was held by soldiers on both sides of the conflict and a fitting thank-you from those American officers whose current freedom was owed to the general's courtesy at the outset of the war in the now burned-out officers' mess at Fort George.

CHAPTER 7

The Frenchman's Creek Fiasco, November 29, 1812

A victory had been won at Queenston, but it had been bought at the price of losing the one individual with the skills and personality to conduct the British war effort with any sort of vigour. General Sheaffe was a competent officer, but was generally considered by his own subordinates as a martinet, focusing on the minutia of military service to the detriment of larger strategic considerations. To the civilian administration of the colony he proved officious, offensive, and totally without the dynamic leadership qualities of his predecessor, General Brock. Nor did he have the fortitude to circumvent Prevost's directives for a quiet defensive posture in dealing with the Americans. As a result, instead of launching an immediate counteroffensive against the shattered American forces, Sheaffe agreed to a three-day armistice, which actually stretched on until mid-November, frittering away his temporary military advantage and allowing the badly demoralized Americans to recover and plan yet another invasion.

On the American side, the debacle of Queenston inevitably led to the resignation of Stephen Van Rensselaer, much to the pleasure of his political opponent Daniel Tompkins, who was now certain of being re-elected as governor. Not to mention the smug satisfaction of Brigadier General Alexander Smyth, who was subsequently appointed as commander of the "Army of the Centre" by Dearborn. No court martial or enquiry was ever held over the mutinous behaviour of Smyth, the shambles of the invasion, or the wholesale failure of a militia regimental system that legally permitted troops to refuse their officer's orders.

Having successfully eliminated Van Rensselaer as his commanding officer and succeeded to his position, Smyth went on to undermine General Dearborn by applying directly to Secretary of War Eustis for an independent command and demanding substantial reinforcements of men, equipment, and supplies. In return, he bombastically promised to pursue an aggressive campaign on the far side of the Niagara that would sweep the defenders away at a stroke. In reality, Smyth's command was in serious trouble. Many of his officers considered Smyth's refusal to work with Van Rensselaer as a betrayal and spoke quietly of the need for a change of command. In addition, an official inspection of the regular and militia regiments stationed at Buffalo revealed a shocking state of deficiencies in the army's organization, as exampled by that of the Fourteenth Regiment, commanded by Colonel W.H. Winder:

> The Colonel and Lieut-Colonel appear to have taken great pains to acquire a knowledge of the duties of their stations. The company officers are almost as ignorant of their duty as when they entered service. The non-commissioned officers and privates are generally only tolerably good recruits.... The arms of this regiment are in infamously bad order. They appear to be old muskets that have probably been bought up at reduced prices by the contractors ... and are now placed in the hands of men who are almost within gunshot of the enemy ... some of the cartridges are said to have been made up in 1794.... All the men are without coats and many without shoes or stocking's and have been obliged to mount guard ... barefooted and in their linen jackets and overalls.... The regiment is composed entirely of recruits. They seem to be almost as ignorant of their duty as if they had never seen a camp and scarcely know on what shoulder to carry the musket ... and if taken into action in their present state will prove more dangerous to themselves than their enemy.[1]

— Captain William King, Assistant Inspector, October 5, 1812

Additional problems came with the fact that the defeat at Queenston had led to wholesale desertions from the ranks of the New York militia, to the point where some companies had more officers than men. Nor were the regular troops immune from discontent, as the Fifth and Twenty-third Infantry regiments mutinied when their pay was not forthcoming.

Seemingly blind to these disaffections and critical problems, Smyth continued his policy of issuing grandiose proclamations that decreed that victory over Sheaffe and his forces was all but complete:

General Order to the Soldiers of the Army of the Centre ...

Companions in Arms!

The time is at hand when you will cross the stream of Niagara to conquer Canada and to secure the peace of the American frontier. You will enter a country that is to be one of the United States. You will arrive among a people who are to become your fellow-citizens. It is not against them that we come to make war. It is against that government which holds them as vassals ... Soldiers! You are amply provided for war. You are superior in number to the enemy. Your personal strength and activity are greater. Your weapons are longer. The regular soldiers of the enemy are generally old men, whose best years have been spent in the sickly climate of the West Indies. They will not be able to stand before you, when you charge with the bayonet.... It is in your power to retrieve the honor of your country; and to cover yourselves with glory.[2]

— Brigadier General Smyth,
November 17, 1812

For his part, General Sheaffe took the success of Queenston and the subsequent armistice as an opportunity for calling out additional regiments of militia for patrol and garrison duties along the Niagara frontier and Grand River valley. Away from the front, Sheaffe also sought to eliminate any potential threat from the pro-American segment of the population by issuing a proclamation directing all citizens of the United States to quit the province by the end of the year, unless they were prepared to forswear their former country and take an oath of allegiance to the Crown.

Convinced that Smyth would attempt to outflank his defences with an attack at either Fort George or Fort Erie, Sheaffe awaited the termination of the armistice on November 20. He then tried to pre-empt the American plans by undertaking an artillery barrage from his guns at Fort George and detached earthworks. This cannonade was readily responded to by the American batteries erected along their side of the river, and throughout November 21, 1812, the opposing batteries pounded away at each other and their surrounding structures. By the end of the day, this extensive firefight could only be credited with having set fire to several buildings with hot-shot, inflicting a few casualties on both sides, and causing a lot of gunpowder to be burned. It did, however, produce two stories that entered local folklore on the American side. The first related to the way the officers and crews of the Salt Battery at Youngstown solved a supply problem during the exchange: "These two officers [Lieutenant John Gansevoort and Lieutenant Hains (First Regiment U.S. Artillery)] and their men in the warmest part of the cannonading, having fired away all their cartridges cut up their flannel waistcoats and shirts and the soldiers their trowsers, to supply their guns."[3] (Lieutenant Colonel McFeeley to Brigadier General Smyth.) In the second story, the garrison at Fort Niagara had the help of a Mrs. Fanny Doyle, the wife of Private Andrew Doyle (First U.S. Artillery Regiment) who had been captured at Queenston the previous month and was now a prisoner on his way to Quebec. Mrs. Doyle served valiantly throughout the day's action, coming under heavy fire as she helped to load and fire a 6-pounder cannon that was mounted on the fort's mess-house roof.[4]

Elsewhere along the frontier, Sheaffe was hard-pressed to find sufficient troops to secure the exposed riverbank from further American incursions and was forced to divide his force into pockets of men, each guarding extended lengths of the riverbank. As a result, when the Americans attempted another invasion, the only force covering the actual landing point near Fort Erie were the reduced detachments from the 41st and 49th Regiments, backed by a single Royal Artillery and two militia artillery detachments. On November 25, 1812, Smyth planned to use over seventy boats, each capable of carrying a hundred men, supported by ten scows, each capable of carrying complete gun teams, limbers, and crew, in order to transport 3,000 men across the Niagara at Black Rock. This assault was designed to swamp the defenders and overrun their positions before reinforcements could be brought up from Chippawa. However, the commander of the proposed invasion (Colonel Winder) was so concerned that an epidemic of pneumonia had broken out only three days before and had already killed over 200 men, with 400 more showing symptoms of the disease, that on November 25 he wrote to Smyth asking for a postponement: "Sir ... the indisposition of the officers to cross is such, and the real difficulties for the want of a little preparatory arrangement, that I fear the issue will be disgraceful and fatal. I would venture to recommend a delay of the expedition."[5]

Calling off this attack, Smyth revised his plans and on the morning of the 26th sent a flag of truce over to the British, ostensibly demanding an immediate surrender, but in reality as an opportunity to make a reconnaissance of the proposed landing points for his new operation. This attack was to be a smaller-scale sortie, designed to eliminate the British batteries along the riverbank and secure a bridgehead before following it up with a larger assault and invasion force. Inevitably, on November 27, 1812, Smyth prefaced his planned attack with yet another proclamation:

> Friends of your country! The moment you have wished for has arrived. Think of your country's honor lost, her rights trampled on, her sons enslaved, and her infants perishing by the hatchet. Be strong! Be brave! And let the ruffian power of the British King cease on this continent….[6]

Around 3:00 a.m. on Saturday November 28, 1812, a force of around 420 troops pushed out into the icy water of the upper Niagara River and pulled for the far shore.[7] The attack was planned to consist of two assault groups, taken from the commands of Colonel William H. Winder and Lieutenant Colonel Charles G. Boerstler, supported by sailors detached from several boats docked at Buffalo. Winder's target, under the joint field command of Captain William King (Fourteenth Infantry) and Lieutenant Samuel Angus (U.S. Navy), was to eliminate the three artillery batteries opposite Black Rock, just below Fort Erie; while Boerstler's target was further downriver at the bridge over Frenchman's Creek. By this it was hoped that the invaders could cut off communications with Sheaffe's troops stationed at Chippawa while providing a secure bridgehead for the main American force to link up with King's force and establish a foothold in Upper Canada.

Under cover of the darkness, King and Angus's troops initially rowed upriver, keeping close to the American riverbank, before moving out into the open water and allowing the current to bring them down onto the Canadian shore. In the darkness, the boats manned by the soldiers found the current difficult to manage and became scattered, while the boats under Lieutenant Angus and his more experienced naval party moved ahead of the pack. Approaching the shoreline, Angus's boats were detected and fired upon by a detachment of some thirty-five men of Lieutenant Lamont's 49th Regiment at what was referred to as the "Red House." This was immediately supported by fire from the gun battery adjacent to the Red House and manned by a detachment of Royal Artillerymen under Lieutenant King (Royal Artillery). Suffering casualties and with one of his craft holed by a cannon ball, Angus's naval unit landed and, without waiting for additional support, made a direct assault

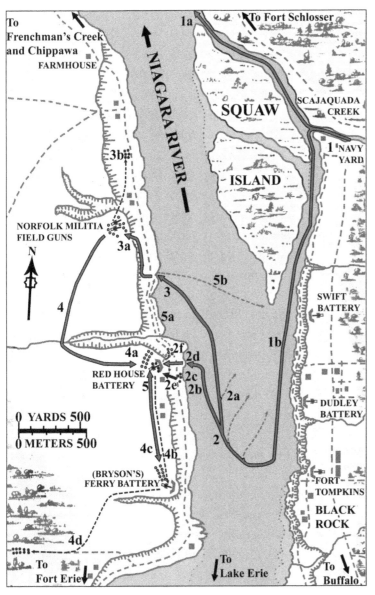

The first American force lands and overruns the British battery positions near Fort Erie.

3:00 a.m. – 4:30 a.m.

1. U.S. forces leave the Navy Yard in Scajaquada Creek (1) and divide into two groups. Lieutenant Colonel Boerstler's flotilla (eleven boats) move north with the current, heading for Frenchman's Creek (1a). Captain King's/Lieutenant Angus' detachments (ten boats) row upriver, against the current, hugging the riverbank (1b).

2. During the crossing of the Niagara River, the King/Angus force becomes separated in the darkness (2), with some boats abandoning the enterprise and returning to their own side of the river (2a). In the boats continuing the attack, the boats with naval crews pull ahead, are detected (2b), and are fired on by a detachment of the 49th Regiment (Lieutenant Lamont) (2c). Under fire, Angus's sailors land and make a frontal assault on the "Red House" battery (2d). Moving into the battery (2e), Lamont's soldiers and the artillerymen drive off Angus's men (2f).

3. Captain King's boats land undetected further downstream (3), attack the Norfolk Militia artillery position (3a) and drive off the militia crews (3b).

4. Advancing south (4), King's force is mistaken for reinforcements by the defenders at the "Red House" battery and are thus able to attack it from the rear (4a). Following

a fierce hand-to-hand fight, the British survivors retreat toward Bryson's battery (4b), shortly afterward pursued by King's men (4c). King's detachment finds the battery spiked and abandoned, with the defenders having already retreated inland (4d).

5. King's detachment returns (5) to link up with Angus's sailors at the Red House battery, only to find them already gone (5a), having taking with them all of the boats (5b).

AMERICAN FORCES, FORT ERIE-FRENCHMAN'S CREEK ACTION, NOVEMBER 28, 1812[7]

Fourteenth Regiment (Lieutenant Colonel Boerstler), 200 Rank and File
Fourteenth Regiment, detachment (Captain King), 150 Rank and File
U.S Navy volunteers (Lieutenant Angus), 70 Sailors

(N.B. Subsequent British accounts report that three sergeants and thirty-one Rank and File, identified as being from the Fifth, Twelfth, Thirteenth, Fourteenth, and Twentieth Infantry Regiments, were amongst those taken prisoner in Captain King's detachment.)

BRITISH/CANADIAN/NATIVE FORCES, FORT ERIE-FRENCHMAN'S CREEK ACTION, NOVEMBER 28, 1812

Fort Erie Garrison (Major Ormsby)

49th Regiment (Major Ormsby), 80 Rank and File
Royal Newfoundland Regiment (Captain Whelan) Light Company, 50 Rank and File

"Ferry" Battery

Norfolk Militia Artillery (Lieutenant Bryson), estimate of 10 Gunners
41st Regiment (Lieutenant McIntyre), 70 Rank and File

"Red House"

49th Regiment (Lieutenant Lamont), 2 Sergeants, 35 Rank and File

"Red House" Battery

Royal Artillery (Lieutenant King), 16 Gunners

Field Guns (in open positions)

1st/2nd Norfolk Militia (Captain Bostwick, Captain Abraham A. Rapelje), estimate of 30–40 Rank and File

Frenchman's Creek Bridge

49th Regiment (Lieutenant Bartley), 2 Sergeants, 35 Rank and File

Chippawa Relief Force (Lieutenant Colonel Clark)

41st Regiment (Captain Saunders), estimate of 80 Rank and File
49th Regiment (Captain Fitzgerald), estimate of 30–40 Rank and File
2nd Lincoln Militia (Captain Hamilton), estimate of 30–40 Rank and File
5th Lincoln Militia (Major Hatt), 300 Rank and File
Militia Artillery (Captain James Kerby), 1 x 6-pounder, estimate of 10 Gunners
Native Warriors (Major Givens), estimate of 30–75 Warriors

upon the battery, while Lieutenant Lamont and his men rushed into the battery to join the artillerymen in fighting off the attack. As the American Naval surgeon, Usher Parsons later remembered and recorded in his diary:

28 November 1813

Our Commander, Lieutenant Angus unwisely volunteered to cross in the night and spike the enemy's cannon.... It was about 3 in the morning when the boats were crossing but were undiscovered and not expected until within 50 rods of the opposite shore. They were hailed and fired upon by the Sentinel. Three cheers were instantly returned by our men mingled with the sound of the enemy's muskets, and in two minutes from the first musket of the Sentinel came a discharge of a 12 pounder, loaded with grape and canister, followed by others. The contents of one of them struck one of the boats and killed & wounded half a dozen. The men sprang from their boats as soon as they struck the shore and it was an incessant crackling of musketry by both sides — and a tremendous yells and uproar of voices mingled with cannon.[8]

In the ensuing fight, the Americans suffered the loss of nine of their twelve officers and twenty-two men killed or wounded before being driven back to the beach. There, they established a defensive position under the cover of the shoreline embankment and continued to fire upon the British in the battery. Meanwhile, Captain King landed three boats undetected slightly further downriver (north) and succeeded in outflanking the northern gun position manned by men of the 1st and 2nd Norfolk militias. Attacking the position from the rear, the Americans charged the guns and, after a fierce hand-to-hand fight, succeeded in overwhelming the position, driving off the militiamen. Having secured this position and spiked the guns, King's force marched upriver (south) seeking to link up with Angus's naval force. Because they were dressed in long blanket coats of the style worn by militia forces in both of the opposing armies, Lieutenant Lamont was initially deceived into believing that the advancing men were the Canadian militia coming to his aid. However, he was soon disabused of that notion when King's men fired a volley into the 49th and charged. After some additional hand-to-hand fighting, Lamont's surviving seventeen men were forced to retire south toward Lieutenant Bryson's battery, leaving their wounded behind to be taken prisoner. Capturing the Red House battery and linking up with Angus's troops, King's force also headed for Bryson's battery, only to find that the gun's crew and its covering detachment of infantry from the 41st Regiment, not knowing of the relatively weak strength of the American force, had already spiked their gun and abandoned the position. Having suffered several casualties, King now looked for the remaining boats of his flotilla to continue his mission, but none appeared out of the darkness, either because they had been swept too far downstream by the strong current or had abandoned the attempt to land once the element of surprise had been lost. Having succeeded in his assigned objectives, King and his men returned to their landing ground, only to find that the naval unit had also gone, abandoning their own damaged boats and taking King's to transport themselves and the wounded back to Black Rock, leaving Captain King and the remains of his detachment stranded on the enemy's shore.

Meanwhile at Fort Erie, the commanding officer, Major Ormsby (49th Regiment), responded to the sounds of gunfire by leading a detachment of about eighty rank and file of the 49th in a circuitous route toward the batteries, avoiding the main riverside road that was potentially occupied by an enemy force of unknown size. Receiving information of the capture of the guns from Lieutenant Bryson, Ormsby changed his line of march and cut across the open fields behind the riverbank road, with the intention of collecting additional troops from a detachment of the 49th under Lieutenant Bartley before advancing on the enemy from downriver (north). Approaching this position, however, he found that they too had been involved in a firefight and forced to retire after suffering several casualties.

The source of these casualties was the second flotilla of eleven boats, containing some 250 men under Lieutenant Colonel Boerstler. This assault had fared even less well in their initial approach to the Canadian shore as they came under heavy fire from Bartley's troops, one of whom, John Chapman, later wrote the following account:

> … a large number of bateaux came over filled with men to make an attack upon us. One of them had got near the British shore before we perceived them. We rushed up in double-quick time & began to fire upon them with muskets, but by the time we had fired five or six times, a six-pounder was brought up & fired into them. Three or four of the boats were destroyed, & terrible havoc was made among the men that landed. Our officers gave the command to cease firing, but … the men were greatly exasperated & fired several times after this command had been given.[9]

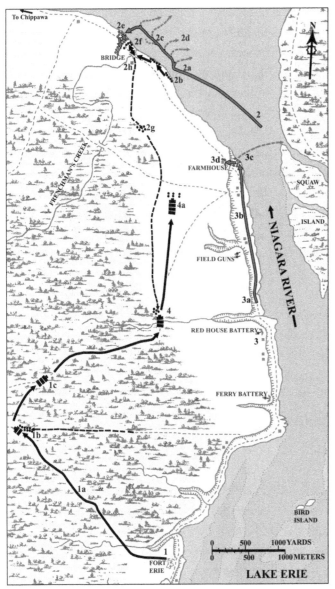

The second American force captures the bridge at Frenchman's Creek, while the British force from Fort Erie march to retake the bridge and reopen communications with Chippawa.

4:00 a.m. – 5:00 a.m.

1. Hearing gunfire from the riverside batteries, Major Ormsby at Fort Erie (1) leads a strong detachment on a wide detour to approach the gun positions from the cover of the forest (1a). Meeting the retreating detachments from the batteries (1b), Ormsby changes his line-of-march, heading for Frenchman's Creek to get additional reinforcements (1c).

2. Lieutenant Colonel Boerstler's flotilla (2) is detected upon their approach to Frenchman's Creek (2a) and is fired upon by Lieutenant Bartley's troops (2b). Moving downstream while under a heavy fire and with at least two boats sunk (2c), most of the remaining boats abandon the crossing and retreat (2d). The remaining troops of Boerstler's force land (2e) and are immediately engaged by Bartley's unit (2f). Overwhelmed, the defenders are forced to retreat (2g), leaving the bridge in American hands (2h).

3. Captain King leaves behind guards on the riverside guns (3) while the remainder of his stranded force moves downriver, searching for boats to make their crossing (3a, 3b). Locating two small skiffs, King sends part of his force back with the wounded and prisoners (3c), while he and the remainder occupy a nearby farmhouse (3d) to await the boats' return.

136

4. Lieutenant Bartley's retreating detachment meets Major Ormsby's force (4), informing him of the capture of the bridge. Ormsby moves on Frenchman's Creek to retake the bridge and re-open communications with Chippawa (4a).

After being under fire for almost twenty minutes, with two boats sunk and several others holed, the majority of the assault wave abandoned the crossing and retired to their own shore, bailing for all they were worth. The remaining boats, containing a force of perhaps 150 troops, completed their crossing, landed, and advanced on the British defenders. In a sharp skirmish, these Americans forced Bartley's surviving men to retreat back (south) over the bridge and took occupation of the vital crossing. However, in total darkness, and without guides or any knowledge of how strong the enemy forces were, Boerstler's troops failed to advance as planned to link up with King's detachment. Instead, Boerstler retired to his landing ground, while leaving behind a detachment with orders to destroy the bridge.

At the same time, King's landing party, depleted by casualties and swollen by prisoners, was attempting to solve its predicament of being stranded on the enemy's shore by searching the shoreline for alternate transport. Unable to locate any boats around the ferry dock, King left detachments to guard the captured batteries and marched north, attempting to reach Boerstler's position. After more than half an hour of marching around in the darkness without contacting Boerstler, King's men finally came across two small boats pulled up on shore. Recognizing that no hope of success for the mission remained, King ordered that his wounded, the British prisoners, and then as many men as possible fill the boats and cross to the American side, while he remained with the rest to hold onto the beachhead from a nearby house until the boats could return and take them off.

Notified of the Americans' capture of the bridge by Bartley's retreating detachment, Ormsby decided to advance on Boerstler's position to reopen communications with Chippawa and the relief force that would surely arrive, as Bartley had already dispatched a warning to Chippawa as soon as the American intentions were determined. Approaching the bridge at Frenchman's Creek, the British again came under fire, this time from the picket guard covering the small demolition team, who were using their bare hands and bayonets in an attempt to destroy the bridge (as the proper tools for the work had been left in the boats). Coming under increasingly heavy return fire from the advancing British, the small American detachment abandoned their efforts and retreated into the darkness to effect their escape. Reaching the beach, they found that upon hearing the sounds of gunfire, Boerstler and his troops had already embarked and quit the Canadian side of the river, leaving them stranded and alone. Having regained the bridge and unable to see his enemy, Ormby acted with caution by holding the bridge and waiting for the approaching daylight to better assess the situation. At dawn, Ormsby's detachment was augmented by a relief force from Chippawa under Lieutenant Colonel Thomas Clark. Together, the combined units, under the overall command of Lieutenant Colonel Cecil Bisshopp, captured the abandoned Americans and secured the riverbank at Frenchman's Creek before moving toward Fort Erie and the remaining scattered remnants of King's troops. Seeing the overwhelming number of enemy troops before them, Captain King and his party of thirty-eight men were left with no option but to surrender.

With their communication lines secure, Bisshopp's column advanced on Fort Erie. Bands of Native warriors augmented the column and the combined force easily retook the batteries from their American captors, only to see a fresh wave of boats approaching the Canadian shore. This new force, taken from Colonel Winder's command, was attempting a crossing in support of King and Boerstler's landing and the intended invasion. However, a few volleys from a quickly formed British line-of-battle and associated field artillery pieces persuaded the Americans to come about and pull out of range, but not before suffering between six to ten killed and

The British retake the bridge at Frenchman's Creek and link up with the relief column from Chippawa before advancing to capture Captain King's stranded troops and retaking the riverside batteries.

5:00 a.m. – 6:30 a.m.

1. Ormsby's force (1) drives off the few Americans at the Frenchman's Creek bridge (1a), who retreat to their landing point (1b) only to find they have been abandoned by Boerstler, who is already retreating across the river (1c).

2. Bisshopp's relief column from Chippawa arrives at dawn (2), captures the abandoned Americans, and unites with Ormsby (2a).

3. The combined British/Canadian force advance on the riverside batteries to recapture them (3) and come across King's unit at the farmhouse (3a). Surrounded, King surrenders, while his relief boats, seeing the British at the farmhouse, abandon their return trip (3b).

twenty-two wounded.[10] Upon inspection, all of the guns in the batteries were found to have been dismounted and spiked but were otherwise undamaged. Without delay, Bisshopp ordered a militia officer, Captain James Kerby (2nd Lincoln Militia Artillery), to oversee the restoration of the barrels to firing condition and the manning of the guns in case the Americans made another assault

On the American side of the river, Smyth watched the remnants of his scheme filter back

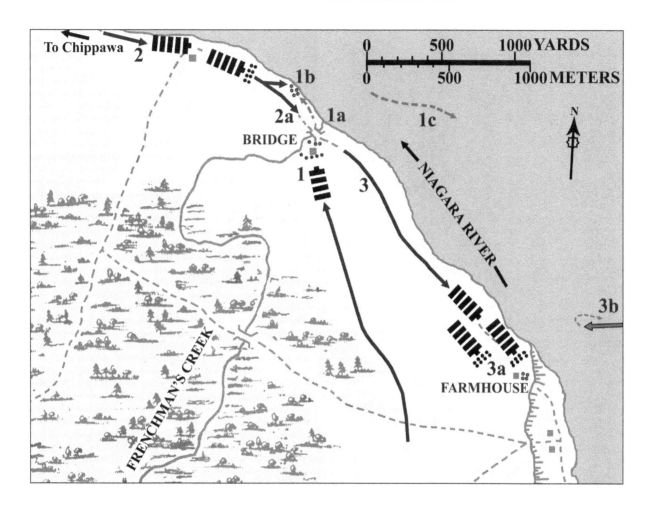

into camp.*[11] These included three of Angus's sailors, who had become separated from their unit during the night and hidden until daylight allowed them to locate a small skiff. They then set fire to three civilian houses at the ferry dock and rowed back across the river, fully expecting to be hailed as heroes. Instead, they were arrested and severely censured for having destroyed private property and causing a hardening of attitudes for revenge on the part of the Canadians. Despite this

**ESTIMATE OF CASUALTIES,
FORT ERIE – FRENCHMAN'S CREEK ACTION,
NOVEMBER 28, 1812**[11]

British Regulars

Killed:	13 Rank and File
Wounded:	2 Officers, 3 Sergeants, 24 Rank and File
Missing/Prisoners:	3 Drummers, 21 Rank and File

Canadian Militias

Killed:	1 Sergeant, 1 Rank and File
Wounded:	2 Officers, 1 Sergeant, 27 Rank and File
Missing/Prisoners:	6 Rank and File

American Regulars

Killed:	Due to losses while crossing the river no accurate account is recorded, estimate of 30–100
Missing/Prisoners:	3 Officers, 3 Sergeants, 49 Rank and File

American Navy

Killed:	5 All Ranks recorded, with an estimate of up to 15
Wounded:	20 All Ranks recorded, with an estimate of up to 30
Missing/Prisoners:	3 Sailors

military humiliation, and the fact that the enemy was now fully alerted and ready, Smyth had a force of men embark in boats in full view of the enemy and then sent across a repeat of his previous demand, that Fort Erie and the troops defending it should surrender immediately "to spare further effusion of blood."[12] On the other side of the river, with his batteries once more in action and with a sizeable force of defenders, Bisshopp ignored Smyth's bombastic demands and later had the satisfaction of watching the Americans unload their troops and march away from the boats — all without a shot being fired.

The following day, Smyth ordered up the detachments of troops that had been sent down-river to the Navy Yard only the night before, and demanded the completion of repairs to his depleted supply of boats in order that another assault could take place during the night of November 30–December 1, 1812. By now Smyth's credibility had totally evaporated and, once again, units of the militia refused to participate in any actions beyond their State lines. Even the regular troops procrastinated in the loading of the boats so that by the time the supposed invasion force was embarked, the sun had risen and the fleet would have been an easy target for every musket and cannon on the Canadian side of the river. Totally frustrated in his schemes, Smyth held a council of his officers (that is to say, his regular army officers, as the militia commanders were deliberately snubbed and excluded from the meeting), which concluded that conducting further offensive operations was an impossibility. As a result, Smyth abandoned the assault, blaming everyone but himself for the debacle.

Discipline in the American Army of the Centre then effectively disintegrated and entire companies of men simply deserted in disgust. Smyth was burnt in effigy by mobs of infuriated militiamen, while others went searching for their erstwhile commander, calling for a lynching. According to the diary of Naval surgeon, Usher Parsons:

Monday Nov. 30

The army returned in the course of the day to the Navy Yard, embarked in the boats long after dark with the professed object of going down to Fort Schlosser to cross.

Tuesday Dec. 1

The army did not descend the river but this morning rowed above Squaw Island under the pretence of crossing when all were suddenly and unexpectedly ordered to debark. This enraged the soldiers against Gen'l Smyth, particularly the volunteers. And when he retired to his camp, advertisements were posted offering 1000 dollars for him, dead or alive. All of the volunteers commenced firing in the air which induced the enemy to think they were firing among ourselves and three cheers were given by them expressive of ridicule and contempt.[13]

Brigadier General Porter, previously a supporter of Smyth in the removal of Van Rensselaer, did an about-face and repudiated Smyth's official report on the debacle. He also publicly called his senior officer a poltroon, scoundrel, and coward, prompting a subsequent face-saving duel in which neither party suffered a scratch. Nevertheless, Smyth was effectively disgraced and within a week was forced to decamp from his own army in fear for his life as unhappy soldiers took potshots in his general direction. He was subsequently "disbanded" from the army (which was a face-saving term used by the army to cover up the otherwise embarrassing need to hold a court martial or official enquiry) whereupon he retired to his home in Virginia, where he sat out the remainder of the war, writing his self-justifying memoirs for posterity.

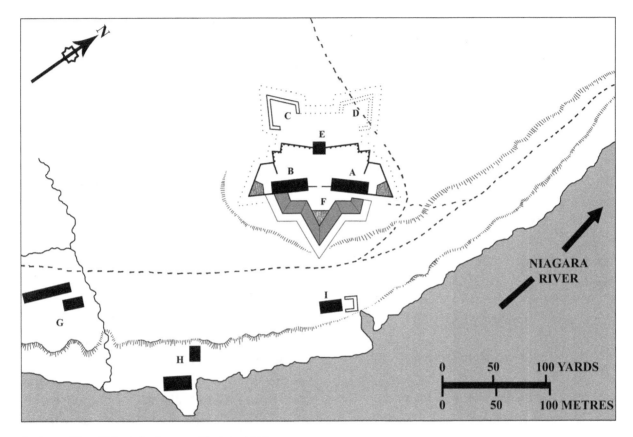

A plan of Fort Erie as it appeared in late 1812.

A	Northeast two-storey stone "Mess" House
B	Southeast two-storey "Mess" House
C	Southwest bastion, only consisting of a stone foundation to ground level
D	Northwest bastion foundation trace, no construction work
E	Western wooden blockhouse in the western wooden picket wall
F	East artillery platform
G, H, I	Civilian and Military warehouses

Above: Even today the isolated position of the garrison of Fort Erie in winter is clearly seen.

Politically, the ramifications of the litany of military failures in 1812 shook the American political administration. President Madison held onto his office in the autumnal elections, but was forced to remove Dr. Eustis as secretary of war on December 3, 1812. In his place, Madison offered the post to several senior politicians, but none of them would touch the job. Eventually a former senator and brigadier-general of militia, John Armstrong, was appointed. Militarily, the administration's claims of having an army, supposedly fully equipped and trained to fight and win a war against the vastly more experienced British army, had been exposed as cruel joke, while its incompetent leadership had become the butt of vitriolic lampoons and political cartoons within the American press. Furthermore, the balloon of myth that had been created during the Revolution, expounding the value of the "Minuteman" militia as the backbone of the "American" army, was now effectively popped. Nevertheless, while several American senior officers thought that a wholesale overhaul of the military system was urgently needed, the political and military leadership was not so perceptive and failed

U.S. Secretary of War John Armstrong, who reluctantly accepted the appointment of secretary of war in replacement of the inept Dr. Eustis, but who subsequently failed to improve the record of the American military in the year to come.

to learn from these disasters, thus creating the conditions for further failures in the future.

On the other side of the border, the New Year's loyal toasts given by the residents of Upper Canada were made with additional fervour this season. By their reckoning, they had:

- been forced into a war for which they were unprepared and under-supplied in military manpower and equipment;
- been dismissed as potentially treasonous and expendable by their own governor in Quebec; and
- defeated three American invasion attempts.

With these "facts" before them, some of the more devout amongst the populace believed that the only obvious answer to the question of why they were not now living under an American flag was nothing less than divine intervention on their behalf.

On the other hand, while equally pleased with the results of the year's actions, the more objective of the civilian leadership and military commanders saw things in a more sober light; starting with the recognition that the war was only just beginning. Furthermore, the existing manpower reserves, not to mention the supplies of military food, ammunition, clothing, and equipment, were all severely depleted as a result of the previous year's campaigning. As a result, until such time as these vital resources could be replaced, it would be practically impossible to consider pursuing any form of offensive action in early 1813. Then there was the problem that the civilian population still contained a sizeable proportion of pro-American sympathizers, headed by several members of the current provincial legislature. But perhaps most serious, in their judgement, was the fact that the senior military commander and now provincial administrator, General Sheaffe, although an able battlefield commander and strict disciplinarian over his troops, was far less able to adapt to the political and social manoeuvring required of his new political responsibilities.

As a result, he was unable to hold together the alliances that his predecessor, Brock, had painstakingly forged. Nor could he persuade Prevost to send vitally needed supplies and ammunition for his troops and Native allies, leading an increasing number of his own officers to question his leadership, discontent amongst his Native allies, and calls from certain members of the Upper Canadian Legislature for his replacement. Matters grew so serious that Sheaffe's health deteriorated under the strain of the responsibility and, for a short time in January 1813, the various departmental and administrative functionaries did the real administration of the war effort in Upper Canada. Receiving word

of these troubles in Upper Canada, Prevost took the extraordinary measure of travelling up to York from his headquarters at Quebec during the coldest and worst part of the winter. After meeting with Sheaffe, Prevost went on an inspection tour of the Niagara positions before returning to express his full support and confidence in Sheaffe, temporarily squashing the incipient revolution.

As the winter progressed, the various strategists and campaign planners on both sides of the conflict looked to their maps to determine where the next stage of the fight for control of the Canadas was to take place, once spring had arrived and the new campaign season had begun. The story of which will be told in the second part of this series.

NOTES

ABBREVIATIONS:

LAC: Library and Archives of Canada.

AOO: Archives of Ontario.

CRDH: Ernest Cruikshank, *The Documentary History of the Campaigns upon the Niagara Frontier 1812–1814*, 9 Volumes (Welland, ON: Tribune Press, 1896–1908).

CGMC: Buffalo and Erie County Historical Society Archives, B00-11, A. Conger Goodyear War of 1812 Manuscripts, 1779–1862.

SBD1812: William C.H. Wood, *Select British Documents of the War of 1812* (Toronto: Champlain Society of Canada, 1920).

A star indicates the note refers to a sidebar.

CHAPTER 1 — INTRODUCTION

1. Robert Gourlay, *Statistical Account of Upper Canada Compiled with a View to a Grand System of Emigration*, 2 Volumes (London: Simpkin and Marshall, 1822). Republished by the Social Science Research Council of Canada, S.R. Publishers Ltd., Johnson Reprint Corp., 1966, 34–44.
2. *Ibid.*
3. *Ibid.*
4. *Ibid.*
5. *Ibid.*
6. *Ibid.*
7. *Ibid.*

CHAPTER 2 — BEATING THE DRUMS FOR WAR

1. Proceedings and Debates of the U.S. House of Representatives, 12th Congress, 1st Session, November 1811.
2. Proceedings and Debates of the U.S. House of Representatives, 12th Congress, 1st Session, December 1811.
3. W. James, *A Full and Correct Account of the Military Occurrences of the Late War between Great Britain and the*

United States of America, Vol. 3 (London: William James, 1818), 77–78.

4. *Ibid.*
5. CRDH, Volume 3, 81–82.
6. W. James, *A Full and Correct Account…*, Vol. 3, 77.
*7. LAC, RG8-I: British Military and Naval Records, 1757–1903, Vol. 1,218, 291.
8. *Ibid.*, 305–06.
9. SBD1812, Vol. 1, 169–70.
10. LAC, RG8-I, Miscellaneous Records, 1812–1815, Freer Papers, Vol. 1,707, 3, and CRDH, Vol. 3, 63.

CHAPTER 3 — THE OPENING ROUND, JUNE TO AUGUST 1812

1. Irving Brant, *The Fourth President: A Life of James Madison*, Vol. 6 (Indianapolis & New York: The Bobbs Merrill Company, 1970), 49.
2. Alexander C. Casselman, ed., *Richardson's War of 1812*, Vol. 1 (Toronto: Historical Publishing Co., 1902), facsimile edition by Coles Publishing Co., Toronto, 1974, 15; and SBD1812, 355–57.
3. *Ibid.*
*4. CRDH, Vol. 3, 91.
5. LAC, RG8-I, British Military and Naval Records, 1757–1903, Vol. 1, 218, 345.
6. SBD1812, Vol. 1, 461.
7. *Ibid.*, 461–62.
*8. SBD1812, Vol. 1, 474; and LAC, RG8-I, British Military and Naval Records, 1757–1903, Vol. 1219, 8.
*9. SBD1812, Vol. 1, 469.
*10. *Ibid.*
11. *Ibid.*, 473.
12. *Ibid.*, 487–89.
13. *Ibid.*, 497.
14. Solomon Van Rensselaer, *A Narrative of the Affair at Queenston in the War of 1812* (New York: Leavitt, Lord & Co., 1836), Appendix, 37–38.

CHAPTER 4 — ACTIONS ALONG THE ST. LAWRENCE RIVER, JULY TO DECEMBER 1812

1. AOO, MS 520, Solomon Jones Papers, Petition of William Fraser, et al., July 7, 1812; and *Kingston Gazette*, July 21, 1812.
2. CRDH, Vol.1, 142; and A. Hough, *History of St Lawrence and Franklin Counties, New York, 1760–1814* (Albany NY: Little & Co. 1853), 621.
3. B. Lossing, *Pictorial Field Book of the War of 1812* (New York: Harper and Brothers, 1868), 369–70; and Hough, *History of St Lawrence and Franklin Counties*, 622.
*4. Compilation estimate derived from: AOO, MU527, Duncan Clark Papers, and AOO, MU 2034, *Events in the Military History of the Saint Lawrence River Valley, 1760–1814*; *Kingston Gazette*, September 19, 1812; and Hough, *A History of St. Lawrence and Franklin Counties*, 623–24.
5. CGMC, Vol. 10, Patrick Finan, *Journal of a Voyage to Quebec in the Year 1825, with Recollections of Canada During the Late American War in the Years 1812–13* (Printed by Alexander Peacock, 1828).
6. *Ibid.*
7. LAC, Duncan Clark Papers, MG19.A39, Vol. 3, 66–67.
8. *Ibid.*
9. Casselman, *Richardson's War of 1812*, 104–06.
10. AOO, MS 519, Joel Stone Papers; J. Mackay Hitsman, *The Incredible War of 1812: A Military History* (Toronto: Robin Brass Studio, 1999), revised edition updated by Donald Graves, 96; and T.H.W. Leavitt, *History of Leeds and Grenville Counties from 1749 to 1879* (Brockville, ON, 1879), 38–39.

CHAPTER 5 — THREATS AND COUNTER-THREATS ALONG THE NIAGARA RIVER, JULY TO OCTOBER 1812

1. Solomon Van Rensselaer, *A Narrative of the Affair at Queenston in the War of 1812* (New York: Leavitt, Lord & Co., 1836), Appendix, 37–38.

2. New York State, Historical Monographs, Historical Literature Collection, Papers relating to the War of 1812 on the Niagara Frontier, Anonymous collection, circa 1850; *Reminiscences of Archer Galloway* (Ithaca, NY: Cornell University Library), 23.

*3. Solomon Van Rensselaer, *A Narrative of the Affair at Queenston ...* Appendix, 37–38; Robert Malcomson, *A Very Brilliant Affair, The Battle of Queenston Heights 1812* (Toronto: Robin Brass Studio, 2003), 257–58; and J.L. Thomson, *Historical Sketches of the Late War Between the United States and Great Britain* (Philadelphia: Thomas Delsilver, 1816), 68.

4. F.H. Severence, *The Case of Brigadier General Smyth* (New York State, Historical Monographs, Buffalo Historical Society Publications No. 18, 1941), 220.

5. CRDH, Vol. 3, 232.

6. Solomon Van Rensselaer, *A Narrative of the Affair at Queenston ...*, Appendix, 37–38.

7. George Auchinleck, *A History of the War between Great Britain and the United States of America during the Years 1812, 1813 & 1814* (Toronto: Thomas Maclear, 1853), reprint by Arms & Armour Press and Pendragon House, 1972, 102–03.

*8. Isaac Roach, *Journal of Major Isaac Roach 1812–1824*, reprint of *Pennsylvania Magazine of History and Biography*, July and October 1893, 6–8.

9. *Ibid.*

10. CGMC, Vol. 10, Letter by John Chapman, circa 1853.

11. J. Armstrong, *Notices of the War of 1812* (New York: Wiley & Putnam, 1840), 254; and Solomon Van Rensselaer, *A Narrative of the Affair at Queenston ...*, Appendix, 20.

*12. Solomon Van Rensselaer, *A Narrative of the Affair at Queenston ...*, Appendix, 19, and 43–45.

*13. LAC, RG8-I: British Military and Naval Records, 1757–1903, Vol. 1, 220, 231–34.

14. CRDH., Vol. 4, 64.

*15. Robert Malcomson, *A Very Brilliant Affair...*, 256.

CHAPTER 6 — PLANS GONE WRONG, THE BATTLE OF QUEENSTON HEIGHTS, OCTOBER 13, 1812

1. CGMC, Vol. 7. Armstrong's letter to Lossing re Queenston Heights.

2. *Ibid.*

3. *Ibid.*

4. J. Armstrong, *Notices of the War of 1812*, Vol. 1, 207.

5. *Ibid.*, 104.

6. Niagara Historical Society Papers, No 28 (c.1916), *Recollections of the Late Hon. James Crooks.*

7. CRDH, Vol. 4, 76–78.

8. Carl F. Klinck, *Journal of Major John Norton*, Publication No. 46 (Toronto: Champlain Society of Canada, 1970), 308.

9. Niagara Historical Society Papers, No 28, *Recollections of the Late Hon. James Crooks.*

10. CRDH, Vol. 4, 85–86.

*11. LAC, RG8-I: British Military and Naval Records, 1757–1903, Vol. 1,220, 234; and CRDH, Vol. 4, 76.

CHAPTER 7 — THE FRENCHMAN'S CREEK FIASCO, NOVEMBER 29, 1812

1. CRDH, Vol. 4, 241.

2. F.H. Severence, *The Case of Brigadier General Smyth*, 227–28.

3. CRDH, Vol. 4, 234.

4. *Ibid.*, 234.

5. *Ibid.*, 237

6. F.H. Severence, *The Case of Brigadier General Smyth*, 227–28.

*7. Composite lists derived from:
Benson J. Lossing, *The Pictorial Field Book of the War of 1812*, Chapter 20; LAC, RG8-I: British Military and Naval Records, 1757–1903, Vol. 690, 42; LAC, RG8-I: British Military and Naval Records, 1757–1903, Vol. 1220, 65; and W. James, *A Full and Correct Account of the Military Occurrences ...*, 110–11, 386.

8. CGMC, Vol. 11, Diary of Naval Surgeon, Usher Parsons, Entries for November 28, 1812.

9. J. Armstrong, *Notices of the War of 1812*, Vol. 1, 111; and F.H. Severence, *The Case of Brigadier General Smyth*, 235.

10. *Connecticut Courant*, February 23, 1813.

*11. Composite lists derived from:
Benson J. Lossing, *The Pictorial Field Book of the War of 1812*, Footnote 37; LAC, RG8-I: British Military and Naval Records, 1757–1903, Vol. 690, 42–43; LAC, RG8-I: British Military and Naval Records, 1757–1903, Vol. 1, 220, 65–66; and W. James, *A Full and Correct Account of the Military Occurrences*, 391.

12. CRDH, Vol. 4, 246, 250.

13. CGMC, Vol. 11, Diary of Naval Surgeon Usher Parsons, Entries for November 30 and December 1, 1812.

SELECTED BIBLIOGRAPHY

PRIMARY SOURCES

Archival
1. Library and Archives of Canada
   Manuscript Groups (MG)
      MG10A: U.S. Department of State, War of 1812
         Records.
      MG11(CO42): British Colonial Office, Original
         Correspondence, Canada.
      MG11(CO47): Upper Canada Records, 1764–1836,
         miscellaneous.
      MG13 (WO62): Commissariat Department,
         Miscellaneous Records 1809–1814.
      MG19/A39: Duncan Clark Papers.
      MG24/A9: Sir George Prevost Papers.

   Research Groups (RG)
      RG5-A1: Civil Secretary's Office, Upper Canada
         Sundries, 1791–1867.
      RG8-I: British Military and Naval Records, 1757–
         1903.
      RG9-I: Pre-Confederation Records, Military.

RG10: Indian Department Records.
RG19/E5A: Department of Finance, War of 1812,
   Losses Board.

2. Archives Ontario
      MS35/1: Strachan Papers.
      MS74/R5: Merritt Papers.
      MS501: Thorburn Papers.
      MS58: Band Papers.
      MS500: Street Papers.
      MS519: Joel Stone Papers.
      MS 520: Solomon Jones Papers.
      MS502/B Series: Nelles Papers.
      MU2099: A.A. Rapelje Papers.
      MU527: Duncan Clark Papers.
      MU2034: Events in the Military History of the Saint
         Lawrence River Valley, 1779–1814.
      MS74.R5: Henry Ruttan Papers.
      Microfilm B91/Reel 1: Table of Statutes, Upper
         Canada Legislature 1792–1840.

3. Metro Toronto Reference Library
      Hagerman, C.: Journal of Christopher Hagerman.

MacDonell, G.: MacDonell Papers.
Prevost Papers, 7 Volumes, S108, Cub 7.

4. Detroit Public Library Archives
Kirby, J.: James Kirby Papers.

5. Buffalo and Erie County Historical Society Archives
A. Conger Goodyear War of 1812 Manuscripts,
1779–1862, Mss. BOO-11, 16 Volumes.

EARLY SECONDARY PUBLICATIONS

Armstrong, J. *Notices of the War of 1812.* New York: Wiley & Putnam, 1840.

Boyd, J.P. *Documents and Facts Relative to Military Events During the Late War.* Privately published, 1816.

Brackenridge, Henry. M. *History of the Late War Between the United States and Great Britain.* Cushing & Jewett, 1817.

Davis, Paris M. *An Authentick History of the Late War Between the United States and Great Britain.* Ithica, NY: Mack & Andrus, 1829.

_____. *The Four Principal Battles of the Late War Between the United States and Great Britain.* Harrisburg, NY: Jacob Baab, 1832.

Hitsman, J.M. *History of the American War of Eighteen Hundred and Twelve.* Philadelphia: W. McCarty, 1816.

James, W. *A Full and Correct Account of the Military Occurrences of the Late War Between Great Britain and the United States of America.* London, UK: William James, 1818.

Johnson, Frederick H. *A Guide for Every Visitor to Niagara Falls.* Niagara Falls: Self-published, 1852.

Lossing, Benson. *Pictorial Field Book of the War of 1812.* New York: Harper and Brothers, 1868.

McCarty, W. *History of the American War of 1812.* Philadelphia: William McCarty & Davis, 1817.

Merritt, William Hamilton. *Journal of Events: Principally on the Detroit & Niagara Frontiers During the War of 1812.*

St. Catharines, ON: Canada West Historical Society, 1863.

Morgan, J.C. *The Emigrant's Guide, With Recollections of Upper and Lower Canada During the Late War Between the United States of America and Great Britain.* London, UK: Longman, Hurst, Rees, Orme & Brown, 1824. New York: Leavitt, Lord & Co., 1836.

O'Connor, T. *An Impartial and Correct History of the War Between the United States of America and Great Britain.* Belfast: Joseph Smyth, 1816. Reprint of the John Low edition, New York, 1815.

"Proceedings and Debates of the House of Representatives of the United States." 12th Congress, 1st Session (1812). U.S. Government Records.

Ripley, E.A. *Facts Relative to the Campaign on the Niagara in 1814.* Boston: Self-published, 1815.

Scott, Winfield. *Memoirs of Lieut.-General Scott.* Sheldon & Co., 1864.

Thomson, J.L. *Historical Sketches of the Late War Between the United States and Great Britain.* Philadelphia: Thomas Delsilver, 1816.

Van Rensselaer, Solomon. *A Narrative of the Affair at Queenston in the War of 1812.*

Wilkinson, J. *Diagrams and Plans Illustrative of the Principal Battles of the War of 1812.* Philadelphia: Self-published, 1815.

SECONDARY SOURCES

Later Secondary Publications

Buell, W. "Military Movements in Eastern Ontario During the War of 1812." *Ontario Historical Society, Papers and Records,* Vol. 10 (1913) and Vol. 17 (1919).

Carnochan, Janet. "Reminiscences of Niagara and St. David's." Niagara Historical Society, Paper No. 20 (1911).

Cruickshank, Ernest. "Campaigns of 1812–1814." Niagara Historical Society, Paper No. 9, 1902.

_____. "Letters of 1812 from the Dominion Archives." Niagara Historical Society, Paper No. 23, 1913.

_____. "A Memoir of Colonel the Honourable James Kerby, His Life in Letters." Welland County Historical Society, Papers and Records, No. 4, 1931.

Currie, Honourable James G. "The Battle of Queenston Heights." Niagara Historical Society, Paper No. 4, 1898.

"Family History and Reminiscences of Early Settlers and Recollections of the War of 1812." Niagara Historical Society, Paper No. 28, 1915.

Government of the United States. "Causes of the Failure of the Army on the Northern Frontier." Report to the House of Representatives, February 2, 1814, 13th Congress, 2nd Session, Military Affairs.

"Historic Houses." Niagara Historical Society, Paper No. 5, 1899.

Kilborn, John. "Accounts of the War of 1812." In Thaddeus W.H. Leavitt. *History of Leeds and Grenville Counties from 1749 to 1879.* Brockville, ON: Recorder Press, 1879.

Leavitt, T.W.H. *History of Leeds and Grenville Counties from 1749 to 1879.* Brockville, ON: Recorder Press, 1879.

Niagara Historical Society Papers, No 28, c.1916. *Recollections of the Late Hon. James Crooks.*

"Reminiscences of Arthur Galloway." Cornell University Library, Ithaca, NY. New York State Historical Monographs, Historical Literature Collection, Anonymous collection, circa 1850.

"Reminiscences of Niagara." Niagara Historical Society, Paper No. 11, 1904.

Severence, F.H., ed. "Papers Relating to the War of 1812 on the Niagara Frontier." *Buffalo Historical Society Publications,* Vol. 5, 1902.

_____."The Case of Brigadier General Alexander Smyth." *Buffalo Historical Society Publications,* Vol. 18, 1941.

Warner, Robert I. "Memoirs of Capt. John Lampman and His Wife Mary Secord." *Welland County Historical Society, Papers and Records,* Vol. 3 (1927), 126–34.

Wright, Ross Pier. "The Burning of Dover." Unpublished manuscript, 1948.

Books

Adams, Henry. *History of the United States of America During the Administrations of Madison.* New York: Library of America, 1986. Reprint of original 1891 volumes.

Antal, Sandy. *A Wampum Denied, Proctor's War of 1812.* Ottawa: Carleton University Press, 1997.

Auchinleck, George. *A History of the War Between Great Britain and the United States of America During the Years 1812, 1813 & 1814.* Toronto: Thomas Maclear, 1853. Reprint by Arms & Armour Press and Pendragon House, 1972.

Babcock, Louis L. *The War of 1812 on the Niagara Frontier, Volume 29.* Buffalo, NY: Buffalo Historical Society Publications, 1927.

Benn, Carl. *The Iroquois in the War of 1812.* Toronto: University of Toronto Press, 1998.

Bingham, Robert. W. *The Cradle of the Queen City: A History of Buffalo to the Incorporation of the City, Volume 31.* Buffalo, NY: Buffalo Historical Society Publications, 1931.

Bowler, R. Arthur, ed. *Essays on the War of 1812 and its Legacy.* Youngstown, NY: Old Fort Niagara Association, 1991.

Brant, Irving. *The Fourth President: A Life of James Madison.* Indianapolis & New York: The Bobbs Merrill Company, 1970.

Casselman, Alexander C., ed. *Richardson's War of 1812.* Toronto: Historical Publishing Co., 1902. Facsimile edition by Coles Publishing Co., Toronto, 1974.

"Contest for the Command of Lake Ontario in 1812 & 1813." Transactions of the Royal Society of Canada, SEC II, Series III, Vol. X.

Cruikshank, Ernest. *The Documentary History of the Campaigns upon the Niagara Frontier in 1812–1814.* Welland, ON: Tribune Press, 1896–1908. 9 Volumes.

Gayler, Hugh J., ed. *Niagara's Changing Landscapes.* Ottawa: Carleton University Press, 1994.

Gilleland, J.C. *History of the Late War Between the United States and Great Britain.* Baltimore: Schaeffer & Maund, 1817.

Gourlay, Robert. *Statistical Account of Upper Canada Compiled with a View to a Grand System of Emigration.* London, UK:

Simpkin and Marshall, 1822. 2 Volumes. Republished by the Social Science Research Council of Canada, S.R. Publishers Ltd., Johnson Reprint Corp, 1966.

Graves, D.E. *Fix Bayonets! A Royal Welch Fusilier at War 1796–1815*. Montreal: Robin Brass Studio, 2006.

Hitsman, J. Mackay. *The Incredible War of 1812: A Military History*. Toronto: Robin Brass Studio, 1999. Revised edition, updated by Donald Graves.

Horsman, R. *The Causes of the War of 1812*. New York: A.S. Barnes and Co., 1962.

Hough, Franklin B. *A History of St. Lawrence and Franklin Counties, New York*. Albany, NY: Little & Co., 1853.

Illustrated Historical Atlas of Norfolk County. Toronto: H. Belden & Co., 1877.

Illustrated Historical Atlas of the Counties of Frontenac, Lennox and Addington. Toronto: J.H. Meachan & Co., 1878.

Illustrated Historical Atlas of the Counties of Hastings & Prince Edward. Toronto: H. Belden & Co., 1878.

Illustrated Historical Atlas of the Counties of Lincoln and Welland. Toronto: H.R. Page, 1876.

Illustrated Historical Atlas of the Counties of Northumberland and Durham. Toronto: H. Belden & Co., 1877.

Illustrated Historical Atlas of the Counties of Stormont, Dundas & Glengarry. Toronto: H. Belden & Co. Toronto, 1879.

Irving, L.H. *Officers of the British Forces in Canada during the War of 1812*. Toronto: Canadian Military Institute, 1908.

"Jarvis Papers." Women's Canadian Historical Society of Toronto Papers and Transactions, Transaction No. 5 (1902), 3–9.

Klinck, Carl F. *Journal of Major John Norton*. Toronto: Champlain Society of Canada, 1970. Publication No. 46.

Mackay, J. *The Incredible War of 1812*. Toronto: University of Toronto, 1965.

Malcomson, Robert. *A Very Brilliant Affair: The Battle of Queenston Heights, 1812*. Toronto: Robin Brass Studio, 2003.

_____. *Lords of the Lake: The Naval War on Lake Ontario, 1812–1814*. Toronto: Robin Brass Studio, 1998.

Ruttan, Henry. *Reminiscences of the Hon. Henry Ruttan: Loyalist Narratives from Upper Canada*. Toronto: Champlain Society, 1946.

Stagg, J.C.A. *Mr. Madison's War: Politics, Diplomacy, and Warfare in the Early American Republic 1783–1830*. Princeton, NJ: Princeton University Press, 1983.

Stanley, George F.G. *The War of 1812: Land Operations*. Toronto: Macmillan of Canada and the Canadian War Museum, 1983.

Wood, William C.H. *Select British Documents of the War of 1812*. Toronto: Champlain Society of Canada, 1920. 3 Volumes.

INDEX

BY THE SAME AUTHOR

Redcoated Ploughboys
The Volunteer Battalion of Incorporated Militia of Upper Canada, 1813–1815
Richard Feltoe
978-1-554889983
$35.00

In 1812, the future of British North America hung in the balance as the United States declared war with the avowed goal of conquering the Canadas and removing British influence from the continent forever.

In response, a corps of men, drawn from every walk of life and social stratum of Upper Canada, stepped forward to defend their fledgling colony by volunteering to serve in the Battalion of Incorporated Militia of Upper Canada. After undergoing rigorous training, and fighting with distinction in numerous skirmishes and battles, it earned the prestigious battle honour "Niagara." The regiment was disbanded at the conclusion of the war, and with the passage of time, its dedicated service and efforts have faded into the dust of histories written about the War of 1812.

Redcoated Ploughboys brings the story of this regiment, and the men who served in it, back to life, revealing a fascinating lost chapter in Canada's early military history.

DUNDURN
www.dundurn.com

Visit us at
Dundurn.com
Definingcanada.ca
@dundurnpress
Facebook.com/dundurnpress